Creating Gender-Fair Schools and Classrooms

Engendering Social Justice 5-13

A Lucky Duck Book

Creating Gender-Fair Schools and Classrooms

Engendering Social Justice 5-13

Lynn Raphael Reed
and Tina Rae

P·C·P
Paul Chapman
Publishing

Paul Chapman Publishing
A SAGE Publications Company
Paul Chapman Publishing
1 Oliver's Yard
55 City Road
London EC1Y 1SP

SAGE Publications Inc.
2455 Teller Road
Thousand Oaks, California 91320

SAGE Publications India Pvt Ltd.
B 1/I 1 Mohan Cooperative Industrial Area
Mathura Road
New Delhi 110 044

SAGE Publications Asia-Pacific Pte Ltd
33 Pekin Street #02-01
Far East Square
Singapore 048763

Commissioning Editor: Barbara Maines

Editorial Team: Wendy Ogden, Sarah Lynch, Mel Maines

Designer: Jess Wright

A catalogue record for this book is available from the British Library

Library of Congress Control Number 2006903953

ISBN 978-1-4129-2357-6

Printed on paper from sustainable resources

Printed in Great Britain by The Cromwell Press Ltd, Trowbridge, Wiltshire

Contents

Introduction

Welcome to this resource. We hope that you will find it challenging, informative and practical in guiding your work around gender with children and adults in education. The text and learning resources draw upon our collective experiences over a number of years of working alongside, and learning from, young people and educational practitioners in a range of educational settings.

Gender aspects of education raise some of the most significant and challenging issues facing us in the 21st century – and it is the intention of this book to offer thought-provoking insights into how to understand these issues and practical strategies to guide the response of staff and learners in 5-13 education. This text looks beyond a narrow focus on just the relative achievement, and under-achievement, of boys and girls in measurable tests and examinations. It addresses concerns about gender and achievement, but within a perspective that prioritises the creation of gender-fair classrooms and schools, where principles of social justice, respect for diversities and inclusion are manifest. What this means in practice we hope will become clear.

From the moment we enter the world, to the moment we leave it, our experiences are shaped by gender. The first question on the birth of a new baby is usually, 'Is it alright?' and the second, 'Is it a boy or a girl?' From that point onwards our identities, our life chances and our experiences are filtered through the lens of gender. Gender shapes the language we use, the concepts we develop and the games we play. It affects our sense of selves and relationship to others, our family dynamics and our educational and employment histories.

It is worth from the outset defining what is meant by the term 'gender'. Like many words with complex and sometimes controversial interpretations, it means different things to different people. While one's 'sex' is primarily biological, and usually ascribed as male or female on the basis of genitalia at birth, 'gender' refers to the social construction of masculinities and femininities. Such gender constructions imply expectations, attitudes, behaviours and opportunities defined as gender appropriate – though what is considered gender appropriate varies between social classes and cultures, and changes over time (Connell 1995). Gender constructs are also relational and tend to be polarised, ie. 'masculinity' is usually defined as oppositional to and different from 'femininity'.

In addition, gender is not just something ascribed to us as passive objects nor is it a fixed and immutable construct. Gender identities are something we actively construct, define, regulate and contest. Gender is something we 'do', not just something we 'have'. For example, the boy in tears after a fall from his bike who is told by his parents that 'boys don't cry', or the girl who enjoys football but is ridiculed by her peers, are both exerting their right to construct and contest gender preconceptions, yet at the same time are being regulated by others in an attempt to maintain some degree of gender conformity.

Mac an Ghaill (1994) begins his book *The Making of Men* with an insightful vignette that illustrates this point well.

> In one secondary school that I taught in, a male student, after hearing that he had passed his exams, gave me bunch of flowers in the school playground. Within a short period of time, the incident was common knowledge in the staffroom and the male teachers responded with heterosexist jokes. At the same time, the student got into a fight in defending himself against homophobic abuse. The headteacher asked me to report to his office, where he informed me that I had gone too far this time. I began to defend myself, claiming that I could not be held responsible for the fight. The headteacher interrupted me to ask what I was talking about. Suddenly I realised the symbolic significance of our playground performance: the exchange of

flowers between two males was institutionally more threatening than the physical violence of the male fight. (p1)

How gender issues are presented today

A concern with gender in education is not new (Arnot et al: 1999). During the 1970s and 1980s, the focus of concern was on the educational experiences of girls, and in particular, their marginalisation in areas of the curriculum. Certain educationalists, working from a feminist perspective, explored how interactions and language in schools and classrooms disadvantaged girls (Arnot and Weiner: 1987; Mahoney: 1985; Spender and Sarah: 1980; Weiner & Arnot: 1987; Walkerdine: 1989). Gender aware strategies at the time attempted to re-shape the curriculum and approaches to teaching and learning to embrace the interests of girls as much as boys for example the Girls into Science and Technology (GIST) initiative.

Such approaches were intended to diversify the aspirations of girls and challenge narrow gender assumptions. As such, they were concerned with broad issues of gender identity and not just attainment in tests and examinations. Whilst there was some interest in applying the same 'anti-sexist' approach to working with boys (Askew and Ross: 1988), concern about the educational experiences of boys was limited, as were studies or strategies that focussed on gender and ethnicities, or gender and special educational needs.

The introduction of the National Curriculum in 1988, and the growing significance of league tables in ranking schools according to their success in standardised assessments, revealed the extent to which girls are outperforming boys in a range of subject areas and throughout all key stages (Arnot et al: 1999). Differential aspects of educational performance between girls and boys have been with us for a very long time (Cohen: 1998). Indeed, the 11+ exam introduced post-war operated with a virtual quota system to ensure that equivalent numbers of boys passed and that girls were not over-represented in grammar schools. What is new is the significance of this information for schools and their reputations. This has led to a situation where the primary focus on gender issues in many educational establishments has shifted dramatically from a broader concern about gender cultures and their effects, to a much narrower and specific focus on the underachievement of boys in measurable tests and related qualifications.

Concerns about attainment

This contemporary focus on the 'underachieving boy' was first articulated publicly by Chris Woodhead, the former Chief HMI. In his annual OfSTED report in 1996 he wrote:

> The gap between the GCSE achievements of girls and boys remains wide. In 1985 some 27.4% of girls and 26.3% of boys were awarded 5 or more grades equivalent to GCSE grades A to C. More recently the equivalent figures have been, respectively, 38.4% and 30.8% in 1990, and 47.8% and 39.1% in 1994, and the provisional figures for 1995 are 48.1% and 39%.

The gender gap at the end of Key Stage 4 was mirrored by a gap in all other key stages. Such statistics have precipitated a flurry of activity aimed at raising the attainment of boys, especially in those subjects with a pronounced gender differential (English, Modern Foreign Languages, the Humanities; Art and Design and Technology). Equal opportunities projects with a broader focus on gender identities and cultures, associated in many cases but not exclusively with concerns about the educational experiences of girls, have been replaced by more instrumental action plans to improve the standard of boys' performance by whatever means necessary (Myers: 2000).

Publishing houses and policy organisations have generated a plethora of texts focussing on the issues from predominantly a male perspective (Bleach: 1998, Frater: 2000, Noble et al: 2001, OfSTED: 2003a, OfSTED 2003b, Wilson: 2003). The DfES have established a website dedicated to issues of gender and achievement (http://www.standards.dfes.gov.uk/genderandachievement) and commissioned a four year Raising Boys' Achievement Project. This project has researched practices in schools where the gender gap was not evident or was narrowing, and developed inter-school interventions through learning triads bringing groups of primary, secondary and special schools together (Younger et al: 2005a, http://www-rba.educ.cam.ac.uk).

Despite all such effort, and notwithstanding the improved results overall, the gender gap has remained fairly constant – indeed, official national statistics claim a slight widening of the gap, (http://www.dfes.gov.uk/trends/) although others have pointed out that proportionally, the rate of improvement for boys is slightly higher (Gorard et al: 2001).

Recent educational statistics reinforce concerns about the national gender gap in attainment at each of the key stages.

Key Stage 1

Percentage of pupils achieving level 2 or above in the Key Stage 1 teacher assessments by gender, 2005

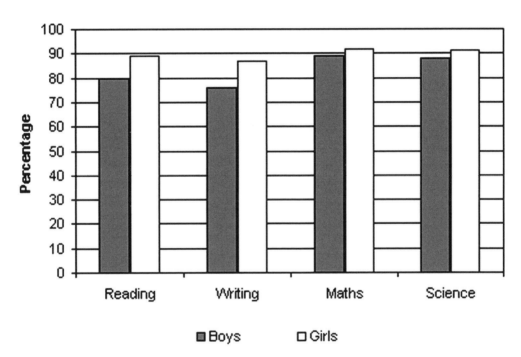

Source: DfES

At Key Stage 1 there is a clear gender gap in performance with a higher percentage of girls achieving the expected level of attainment or above in all subjects than boys. According to teacher assessments, the difference in the proportion of girls and the proportion of boys achieving level 2 or above in 2005 was greatest for writing - 88 per cent of girls compared to 77 per cent of boys. Differences were less significant in science and mathematics. Indeed, at the higher levels of attainment a higher percentage of boys than girls attained level 3 in maths and science.

Key Stage 2

Percentage of pupils achieving level 4 or above in the Key Stage 2 writing test by gender, 2000 to 2005

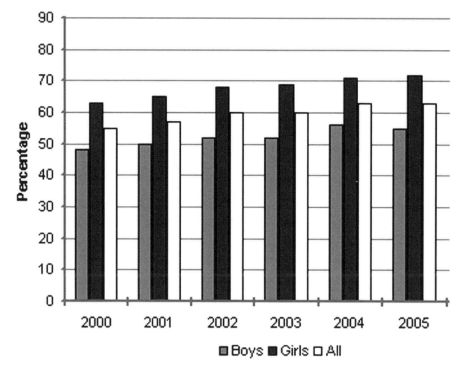

Source: DfES

At Key Stage 2 the levels of attainment overall have risen over the six year period from 2000-2005. However, the difference between the percentage of girls and the percentage of boys achieving level 4 or above in the writing test increased by two points in 2005 to reach 17 percentage points. The proportion of boys achieving level 4 or above in the writing test fell by one percentage point to 55 per cent in 2005, while the proportion of girls achieving level 4 or above in the writing test increased by one percentage point to 72 per cent.

Key Stage 2

Percentage of pupils achieving level 4 or above in the Key Stage 2 reading test by gender, England, 2000 to 2005

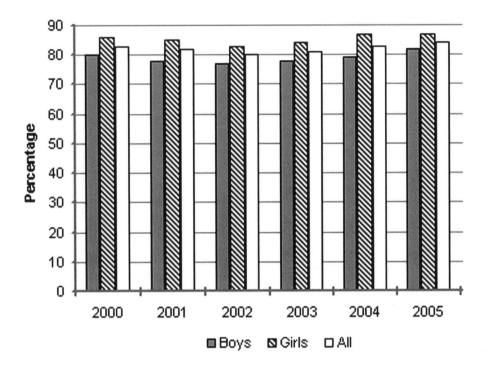

Source: DfES

In reading at Key Stage 2 there appears to have been recent narrowing of the gender gap. The proportion of pupils achieving level 4 or above in the Key Stage 2 reading test increased by one percentage point in 2005 on the previous year to 84 per cent. The difference between the percentage of girls and the percentage of boys achieving level 4 or above in the reading tests fell by 3 points to 5 percentage points in 2005. The proportion of boys achieving level 4 or above in the reading test increased by three percentage points, to 82 per cent in 2005, while the proportion of girls achieving level 4 or above in the reading test remained at 87 per cent.

In mathematics and science at Key Stage 2 equivalent percentages of boys and girls achieved the expected levels, although, again, at the higher levels of attainment boys slightly outperform girls in these subjects.

At Key Stage 3, similar patterns are again in evidence. The percentage of girls achieving level 5 or above was 14 percentage points higher than that for boys in the English tests - the same difference as in 2004. The percentage of girls achieving level 5 or above was one percentage point higher than that for boys in both the mathematics tests and the science tests in 2005.

Key Stage 3

Percentage of pupils achieving level 5 or above in the Key Stage 3 tests by gender, 2005

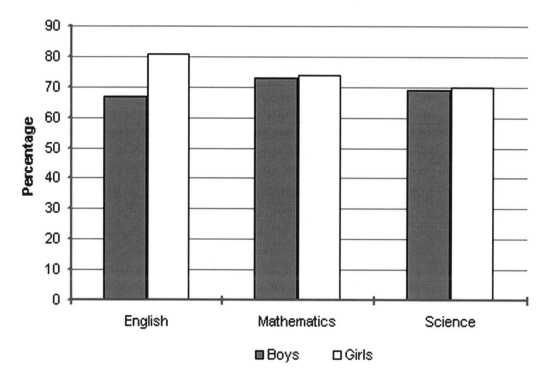

Source: DfES

In teacher assessments for non-core subjects, girls outperformed boys in all subjects except in Physical Education. These results were again within a context of overall improvement of performance.

Key Stage 3

Percentage of pupils achieving level 5 or above in the Key Stage 3 teacher assessments in non-core subjects by gender, 2005

Subject	All	Boys	Girls
History	70	64	76
Geography	70	65	75
Design and Technology	73	66	79
ICT	69	65	74
Art and Design	75	67	83
Music	69	63	75
Modern Foreign Languages	52	44	60
Physical Education	76	77	75

Source: DfES

Such patterns of attainment from Key Stage 1-3 set a trajectory that is sustained through Key Stage 4 and beyond.

Key Stage 4

Percentage of pupils aged 15 achieving 5 or more GCSEs or equivalent at grades A* to C, England, 1994/95 to 2004/05

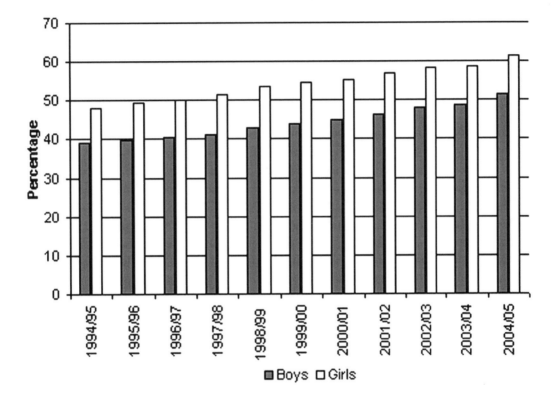

Source: DfES

The percentage of pupils achieving 5 or more GCSE and equivalent grades A* to C, in England increased from 43.5 per cent in 1994/95 to 56.3 per cent in 2004/05. During this time the percentage of girls achieving 5 or more good GCSEs or equivalent has increased by 13.3 points, while the percentage of boys has increased by 12.4 points. Approximately 61% of girls currently achieve 5 A*-C or equivalent, compared to 51% of boys.

Post-16

Percentage of 16-18 year old candidates achieving 2 or more GCE A level passes in schools and FE colleges, England, 1993/94 to 2004/05

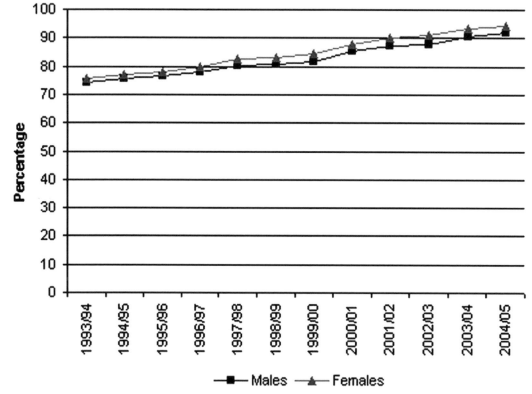

Source: DfES

In 2004/05 there were 277,600 16-18 year olds taking GCE/VCE A/AS level examinations in schools and FE colleges in England. 93.2 per cent of these achieved two or more 'A' level passes, compared to 76.2 per cent in 1994/95. Of these, 94.2 per cent of 16-18 year old females achieved two or more passes, compared with 92.0 per cent of males. The gender gap among 16-18 year olds has widened over the last decade.

Such statistical patterns are reinforced by the fact that more boys than girls leave compulsory education with no qualifications at all, and fewer young men stay on in education or training post-16. The majority of applicants and entrants to Higher Education are also now women (HEFCE: 2005).

Concerns about behaviours

The other way in which the current debate about gender and education is framed relates to concerns about 'challenging behaviours' and the extent to which formal and informal exclusion from education is gendered. Boys are more likely to be reprimanded for their behaviours than girls and to receive fewer rewards or positive affirmations (Warrington et al: 2006; Younger et al: 2005b). Approximately 80% of fixed term and permanent exclusions from secondary school are male with almost all primary exclusions being boys (DfES SFR 23/2005). Boys are over-represented in Special Educational Needs (SEN) provision, with higher levels of learning difficulties and emotional and behavioural needs identified, including specific syndromes, e.g. Attention Deficient Hyperactivity Disorder (ADHD) and Asperger's Syndrome (OECD: 2000). In 2004/05, more than twice the number of boys than girls in schools had statements of SEN and about the double the number of boys than girls were identified as having SEN. Boys outnumber girls in SEN units and special schools (DfES SFR 24/2005).

The trajectory of disaffected behaviours through from primary to secondary schools means the vast majority of pupils who truant are boys and there is a strong link between truanting and crime. Youth Justice Board statistics show a highly gendered pattern of youth offending (Bowles et al: 2005). This includes a worrying statistic that 15% of boys in high crime neighbourhoods report carrying a knife to school (compared to 4% of girls). In a Bristol study, over 75% of 11/12 year old boys believe women should be hit if they make men angry. In July 2000, The Racial and Violent Crime Task Force set up after the Stephen Lawrence enquiry, found that of 8000 incidents of violence dealt with each month, 76% were domestic, 22% racial and 2% homophobic. Recent reports about antisocial youth, gangs wearing 'hoodies' and the issuing of Anti-social Behaviour Orders (ASBOs) has tended to characterise, and demonise, groups of teenage boys in particular.

Finally, statistics about rising suicide rates for young men have been widely reported. For men aged 15 to 24 the suicide rate has doubled in the last 25 years, now standing as the most significant single cause of death of men in this age group – approximately a quarter of all cases. Conversely, the suicide rate for young women is considerably lower and has remained relatively stable over the same period (www.statistics.gov.uk), although suicide attempts are far more common amongst women than men – especially in the under 25 age group. Male suicides appear to be more impulsive and frequently are not foreshadowed by prior discussion or calls for help. In addition, they are often enacted through more violent means. Suicide risk is clearly linked to mental health and self-esteem issues, unemployment, marital breakdown or relationship problems, homophobia and other forms of bullying, drug or alcohol abuse. In addition, the pattern of male suicide indicates some connection with the difficulty many men feel in expressing feelings of inadequacy, exposing vulnerabilities and managing a sense of powerlessness (Coleman: 2004).

A focus on the mental health issues facing men is part of a growing concern about the challenges associated with encouraging men to engage proactively in their own health care and well-being. Testicular cancer, for example, the commonest cancer in men aged 20-34, can have an 85% chance of cure if caught early enough, but young men's resistance to self-examination persists. Reflecting this new concern, a Parliamentary Committee was set up in 2001 – the All Party Group on Men's Health.

What such perspectives conceal

Overall then the terms of the current debate, both in the public eye, and underlying many contemporary educational interventions, have defined a certain construct – the 'underachieving boy' – that commands our attention in a particular way. Indeed there are powerful discourses at play here that shape what we perceive, how we interpret what we see, and how we respond (Raphael Reed: 1999). Some have argued that the current gender discourses around the underachievement of boys represent a contemporary 'moral panic' that acts to channel anxieties relating to changing gender and youth cultures (Epstein et al: 1998).

The concept of discourse is a useful one. Associated with the work of Michel Foucault (1926-1984), discourse refers to the way that knowledge is constituted and inter-related with power, not just at the level of theory (how we think) but also at the level of practices (how we act). In this context, contemporary discourses associated with the 'underachieving boy' are influencing what gets noticed in relation to gender and education, and are shaping the interventions in response. By extension, the dominant discourses exclude or hide certain issues from view.

So what do current perspectives tend to conceal?

Firstly, the focus on the gender gap in favour of girls misrepresents remaining issues of gender and performance for girls in some curriculum areas. A recent Leverhulme longitudinal research study into numeracy development shows a decline in mathematical performance for lower attaining girls since the implementation of the National Numeracy Strategy, with some indication that increased levels of competition, public performance, and mental arithmetic with a focus on the 'right answer' have disadvantaged them (Lucey et al: 2003). Even in curriculum areas where girls are seen to be achieving, for example, in literacy or English, there are some concerns that their compliant engagement with schooled literacies may conceal a lack of confidence at manipulating and deconstructing multimodal texts (Browne: 1999).

Secondly, whilst the dominant construction of the underachieving boy suggests that everything in the garden is rosy for girls and young women, and that the 'future is female' – further enquiry reveals that there are still significant gendered patterns and barriers that impact upon female life chances and opportunities.

A closer look at educational progression post-16 and employment opportunities reveals some interesting patterns. Whilst the gender differentials discussed from KS1 through to post-16 and beyond are apparent, the picture post-16 is more polarised than the generalised statistics suggest. Though more girls are staying on into post-16 education and account for over 50% of 'A' level entries, the gender gap in favour of girls is relatively small. At 'A' level and 'AS' level boys gain very high or very low point scores more often than girls. For boys and girls with similar GCSE point scores, boys appear more likely to achieve high 'A/AS' point scores – particularly candidates with high GCSEs. At degree level there are also some interesting patterns. A slightly higher proportion of men achieve first class degrees than women, but many more graduate with a third class or ordinary degree. At some elite universities such as Oxford and Cambridge, men are twice as likely as women to get firsts, with a higher proportion of women getting lower second class degrees, despite similar grades at intake.

Traditional and differentiated subject choice by gender is still evident when option choices are made. At post-16 boys favour physics, chemistry, maths, economics, geography, design and technology; girls favour sociology, French, English Literature, biology and art, even when they have done well in science and mathematics at GCSE. In vocational subjects, there is a rigid gender divide with males predominating in construction and engineering courses, and girls in health and social care.

Despite the fact that the Sex Discrimination Act was passed 30 years ago, there is also still evidence of a significant 'glass ceiling' operating for women in employment, and low female representation in traditionally male spheres. One area of particular concern is the low representation of women in ICT based careers. Just 33% of managers and 14% of company directors are women (EOC: 2005). Only 32% of head teachers in secondary schools are women – whilst at the same time there is a concentration of women in the less well-paid roles of early years practitioner and learning support. A focus on the underachievement of boys may have affected women teachers' career prospects.

Although female employment is many areas outstrips men, this is frequently in low-paid and part-time work which men are often unwilling to do. A recent report from the EOC confirms that the full-time gender pay gap is 17.1% in favour of men, and the part-time gender pay gap is 38.4% (EOC: 2006). Gender cultures within the family, the interplay between work-home responsibilities, and the long hours culture in the world of work in Britain, still results in women taking the main responsibility for unpaid domestic caring roles combined with part-time employment – although there is an increasing demand from both men and women to be able to strike a healthier and more equitable work-life balance (Women and Work Commission: 2006). Women returning to work after starting a family face the highest 'employment penalty' of any group in society (The Equalities Review: 2006).

Thirdly, current debates tend to characterise boys as a homogenous whole - suggesting all boys are underachieving or disadvantaged. This is far from the case. Undifferentiated figures by gender conceal important differences in achievement by social class. Middle class boys tend to do better than working class girls (though the educational experiences of working class girls have never been high on the policy agenda (Plummer: 2000) notwithstanding current rates of teenage pregnancy amongst the highest in Europe). While social class remains the single most significant contributor to educational outcomes and life chances (Ball et al: 2000), there are also complex and dynamic interplays between other factors as a 'basis for chronic, persistent and unjust inequalities' (The Equalities Review: 2006).

Pupils of Indian and Chinese heritage show a pattern of high attainment compared with other ethnic groups. Pupils of Pakistani, Bangladeshi, Black African and Black Caribbean heritage perform as a percentage below the national average, with Travellers of Irish heritage and Gypsy/Roma pupils achieving extremely poorly. If one takes value added measures into account, the attainment gap does narrow to some extent during compulsory education for some ethnic groups (predominantly Bangladeshi and to a lesser extent Pakistani and Black African) – especially for groups with high proportions of EAL speakers. Black Caribbean pupils have lower value added scores and their performance declines relative to other groups from age 7 onwards (DfES: 2005).

Once intersected with gender, the gender gap is largest for the following four minority ethnic groups: Black Caribbean (15%); pupils of Mixed White and Black African heritage (16%); pupils of mixed White and Black Caribbean heritage (15%) and Bangladeshi pupils (14%). Overall, the educational experiences and outcomes for Black Caribbean boys remains a cause for concern in many local authorities, despite the fact that their rate of improvement in GCSE is currently twice that of White boys.

Exclusion rates are not only gendered but also differentiated by ethnicity. The disproportionate rate of permanent exclusion for minority ethnic pupils has fallen considerably over the last six years. However, Black pupils and pupils of Mixed ethnic origin remain at greatest risk of exclusion, being twice as likely to be excluded from school than White pupils (DfES SFR 23/2005) with Black Caribbean pupils excluded at three times the rate (Parsons et al: 2005).

Whilst there is some correlation between educational outcomes, ethnicity and class – young people from some ethnic groups buck the trend showing little difference in performance between children on Free School Meals (FSM) and others for example, those of Chinese and those of Bangladeshi heritage (The Equalities Review: 2006).

Fourthly, a narrow focus on achievement and examination results underplays other elements of gender experience in schools. The experiences of those young people whose sexual orientation or gender identity challenges the dominant or hegemonic forms of masculinity and femininity are marginalised. Lesbian and gay adults report having been subject to high levels of homophobic bullying while at school with over half contemplating self-harm as a result. A Stonewall survey found that 82% of teachers were aware of incidence of homophobic bullying but only 6% of schools had anti-bullying policies that dealt specifically with these issues (Warwick et al: 2004). Children as young as Key Stage 1 use the term 'gay' pejoratively to regulate the behaviours of others (Browne: 2004).

Girls may be seen to be succeeding at examinations but they are still the recipients of a significant amount of sexual harassment and bullying by boys, as are marginalised and vulnerable boys who do not conform to the dominant 'macho' forms of identity. Girls often find boys' behaviours distracting and observations of classrooms demonstrate continued male domination of space and of teacher time (Francis: 2000). Teachers continue to excuse problematic gender behaviours in the classroom through drawing on a 'boys will be boys' narrative (Kenway and Willis: 1998).

The focus on the underachieving boy can also blind us to considering problematic aspects of girl experiences for example, increases in self-exclusion, poor relationships with teachers, psychological bullying, eating disorders, self-harm and abuse (Besag: 2006; Lloyd: 2005; Osler and Vincent: 2003). The achievement culture itself produces penalties, with increasing evidence that high achieving middle class girls, even at a very young age, experience worrying levels of stress and self-doubt (Lucey: 2001; Walkerdine et al: 2001).

In addition, the disciplinary and punishing effects on young bodies of certain forms of hegemonic masculinity, even for those boys and young men who appear to 'succeed' in such terms, is also of concern. Eating disorders and body image problems affect boys as well as girls – with a link between male eating disorders, athletic prowess, body-building and the quest for physical power and perfection (Langley: 2005; Patterson: 2004).

Finally, the over-determining focus on the achievement of key outcome targets by whatever means necessary leads to a distortion of educational practices. Reputations of schools and Local Authorities in educational league tables mean that teachers tend to prioritise teaching to the test – and commit limited resources to those students on the borderline in a form of 'educational triage' (Gillborn and Youndell: 2000). Other students at this point lose out. While this is most especially pronounced at the end of Key Stage 4, the pattern is replicated at other critical assessment points. There is also some evidence of the increase in authoritarian management and 'poisonous pedagogies' in some settings as pressure and 'zero tolerance' of failure rises (Raphael Reed: 1998a).

Making sense of the issues

Before exploring in more detail what a more inclusive and socially just perspective on gender issues in education might entail, it is worth pausing to consider the implications of some of the most influential paradigms and theories drawn upon to 'explain' current outcomes. This is not about abstract theories – these perspectives for 'making sense' of the issues, inform and influence the practices of policy makers and practitioners alike; they seep into our consciousness and underpin our behaviours. Returning to the concept of discourse, we need to recognise the 'regimes of truth' sustained by such discourses, and make explicit, interrogate and evaluate both taken-for-granted assumptions and critical theories. How we understand the nature of the issues informs the strategies we employ to engage with them.

Biological and psychological perspectives

Ideas of essential natural differences between men and women form one end of a continuum in the 'Nature versus Nurture' debate. This includes an increasing fascination within the general public and mass media with ideas of fundamental differences in the male and female brain. Some claim gender difference in brain hemisphere dominance with left hemisphere functions (associated with logical, visual-spatial and rationalist thought) more developed in men and right hemisphere (associated with language, empathy and intuition) in women. Some argue that women's perceived greater ability to multi-task arises from a more developed corpus callosum facilitating cross-hemisphere functions. Others claim biological difference on an aggression-competition (male) versus compassion-collaboration (female) spectrum based on primitive hunter-gatherer drivers or exposure to testosterone before or after birth. Such ideas resonate with common-sense beliefs rooted in observable behaviours from the early years to beyond (Biddulph: 2003; Gray: 1992; Gurain: 2001; Hannan: 1999).

There are a number of problems with these perspectives. More circumspect reading of the 'seductive science' literature related to essential gender differences reveals contradictory evidence and assertions based on small amounts of data (Browne: 2004). Janet Shibley Hyde (2005) undertook a detailed review of 46 meta-analyses of the literature on gender difference and found overwhelming support for a 'gender similarities hypothesis', ie. males and females are similar on most, though not all, psychological variables and that such variables are profoundly affected by context especially where gender expectations are evident, for example girls in one study who knew they were individually identifiable while playing a war scenario computer game dropped few bombs, but those who felt they were not identifiable dropped more bombs than the boys. She also argues over-inflated claims of gender differences carry substantial costs for both male and female in education, the workplace and relationships.

A more contextualised approach emphasises the impact of nurture and ongoing expectations for cognitive style and learning preferences – without resorting to essential difference. From birth onwards girls and boys are often handled, spoken to and interacted with differently, and are given different toys to play with and books to read. Such differentiated experiences are to some extent reinforced by schools. Paechter (1998) points out that neural connections are strengthened as a result of experience, so given the different experiences that girls and boys are having from birth, some differential impact on cognitive development is likely.

Head (1997) discusses the relationship between gender identity and cognitive style – where boys tend to develop field-independent preferences (such as learning for more abstract, technological and non-relational contexts and purposes), while girls develop field-dependent preferences (such as learning for more embedded, moral and relational contexts and purposes). He also references gender differences in attribution for success and failure, with boys tending to attribute their success to themselves and their failure to others, while girls tend to do the opposite. This is mirrored in social learning theories about 'locus of control' (Rotter: 1982).

Such ideas resonate with contemporary fascination about 'preferred learning styles' (Smith: 1998) and multiple intelligences (Gardner: 1999). In this book, while we urge awareness of strategies that draw upon a range of modes of mediating meaning and engaging learners – and classroom contexts that value attributes across a range of 'intelligences' – we also caution against using these concepts uncritically (Coffield: 2004) or as fixed and reified constructs that 'pigeonhole' learners in the ways that older ideas about IQ and ability have done before (Hart et al: 2004).

Fundamentally this relates to underlying beliefs about learning. If one adopts a predominantly developmentalist approach, associated with the ideas of Piaget, then this implies that children and young people (provided the context is stimulating enough) will unfold through 'natural' stages of development. If one adopts a more social constructivist approach, associated with the ideas of Vygotsky, then this implies a key role for social interaction and intervention to shape and transform children's learning (Wood: 1998).

In relation to gender and learning, the developmentalist approach has a long history of reinforcing gender restrictive expectations, especially in the primary and early years (Walkerdine: 1983) – in part through the tendency to characterise boys as 'bright but naughty', and girls as 'diligent and compliant'. Browne (2004) argues that ideas of 'normal' child development tend to be modelled on white middle class boys with everyone else by implication carrying some deficit. She also argues that even highly regarded approaches to early years education for example, the Reggio Emilia pre-school provision in Italy, fail to engage pro-actively enough with gender oppressive behaviours in children. By contrast, a social constructivist perspective demands that as educators we do not just observe gendered behaviours and preferences, but we engage with them through dialogue and actions to disrupt restrictive patterns and extend the development of the learner.

Sociological and cultural perspectives

Social role theories propose that we develop our sense of ourselves as gendered beings through modelling ourselves on the behaviours of others and responding to positive or negative reinforcement. This led to a raft of gender based interventions flowing from the liberation movements of the late 1960s and 1970s, aimed at altering the socialisation of girls and boys through the provision of alternative stimuli (for example, anti-sexist books, toys and tools). Since the 1975 Sex Discrimination Act, the Equal Opportunities Commission for example has produced many resources aimed at changing the landscape of gender in schools. From this perspective, encouraging girls to play with construction kits and boys to play with dolls should result in the development of non-stereotypical outcomes in childhood and adult life (Arnot et al: 1999). Sex role theories also underpin the call to increase the number of male teachers in primary and early years settings, despite the fact that there is no sound evidence that male teachers necessarily have a more positive influence or that feminisation of teaching is the 'problem' (Ashley and Lee: 2003).

While sex role theories have the advantage of challenging assumptions that gender behaviours are just innate, the limitations of the sex-role socialisation thesis have become increasingly clear. From around the age of four, children exhibit strongly separate gender identities, groups of friends and styles of play. They also invest considerable energy in gender maintenance activities (Lloyd and Duveen: 1992). In light of this, new ways of thinking about the issues need to be explored (Skelton and Francis: 2003):

> Many of the practices recommended in schools' equal opportunity policies today that are intended to redress gender inequalities have their roots in sex role socialization strategies. Yet … these approaches have done little, if anything, to change the ways in which boyhood and girlhood is perceived and judged by adults as well as acted out by children … The question has to be asked as to why this is the case. (p 13)

Children and young adults are not just passive recipients who can be moulded by the behaviourist interventions of others. Rather, they are active and dynamic subjects, formed in the interplay between self and others in specific cultural settings, attempting to exert agency over their own lives. They demonstrate complex and multilayered decisions and choices in terms of their actions, and these change over time and in response to context. More recent approaches to understanding gender formation and practices highlight the concept of multiple and relational gender identities (Blair et al: 1995).

Such ideas are useful for a number of reasons

Firstly, they allow us to recognise that there are multiple versions and ways of being male and female – of 'masculinities' and 'femininities' – and that we should not reduce the experiences of all boys and girls to homogenised and stereotypical singularities (Epstein: 1994; Mirza: 1992; Sewell: 1997). Rather than representing gender identities in terms of simple binary opposites, it is more useful to see them on a continuum. Within this, there is the recognition that there are hierarchies of power that operate in and through various forms of gender identity; for example, some expressions of masculinity (referred to as hegemonic masculinity) assume and assert greater dominance and power than others (Connell: 1995; Mac an Ghaill: 1994).

Secondly, they remind us to look carefully at the processes of interaction through which gender identities are expressed and by which they are sustained. No amount of non-stereotypical role models or anti-sexist materials are going to impact on the living interactions between children and young adults as they utilise gender as a tool in defining themselves and others and in making their mark on the world (Thorne: 1993). This includes children and young adults using gender through verbal and physical interactions to regulate the behaviour of each other and to maintain and defend a sense of self-worth. Indeed as Browne (2004) argues:

> Since the binary gender divide is not 'natural' children have to learn the social practices and signifying systems in circulation in society as a whole that delineate 'female' and 'male' in order to position themselves and others successfully … Adopting a fairly rigid view of what is gender-appropriate reduces the degree of uncertainty surrounding gender categories and in doing so upholds the essentially arbitrary categories that have been constructed through the dominant discourse (p 72).

Gender is also drawn upon in interactions between children and their teachers. Walkerdine and Lucey (1989), for example, describe how two small boys use sexually explicit language when defying their nursery teacher and in doing so seize power by positioning their teacher as a 'powerless object of sexist discourse' (p60). But how gender interactions happen varies significantly according to context including aspects of context associated with social class and ethnicities (Ball et al: 2000; Connolly: 1998; Jackson: 2006; Martino and Pallotta-Chiaroli: 2003).

Successfully doing 'boy-ness' or 'girl-ness' has profound implications for relationships and educational biographies. In many contexts, maintaining one's gender identity effectively places one at odds with the ethos and practices of successful schooling. Indeed many have noted the psychic and physical effort and costs in balancing and negotiating conflicting demands and expectations from different quarters (Frosch et al: 2002; O'Donnell and Sharpe: 2000; Reay: 2002). One implication of this is that we need to listen more carefully and understand more fully what the issues are for children and young adults, both inside and outside schools, as they try to navigate their way through the world.

Thirdly, these ideas encourage us to understand that gender identities are not fixed and immutable, but that they are more fluid and open to change. The challenge in education is to promote effective ways of engaging with gender dynamics in schools and classrooms in such a way as to promote positive change for all (Davies B: 1989; Salisbury and Jackson: 1996). Developing effective interventions is not easy. Both adults and children have much invested in maintaining the status quo. Gendered play, for example, is a means of providing emotional satisfaction and rewards and allows children to explore some of the tensions and contradictions within their gender positions. As Browne (2004) argues:

> Participating in children's role play in order to provide them with opportunities to explore 'alternative ways of being' requires a light and sensitive touch on behalf of the adult. Children will reject moves that require them to relinquish emotionally satisfying positionings. Many boys are also likely to react negatively to suggestions that involve surrendering their power, especially in there is no emotionally satisfying alternative position or version of 'masculinity' (p124).

In light of the challenges, and within the context that encourages a more narrow focus on educational tests, it is not surprising that many educators have begun to retreat from tackling these issues. What we need at this point, are practical examples of how to engage productively with the complexities of gender cultures in our schools and classrooms, and how to assist children in understanding and deconstructing the power of gender over their lives (Davies: 2003; Francis et al: 2002; McNaughton: 2000; Salisbury and Jackson: 1996). Such engagement, we would argue, requires educational practices that are ethical and critical – informed by the principles of inclusion and social justice.

Gender and social justice: an inclusive approach

Rather than a narrow focus on the underachievement of boys in tests and examinations, in this book we are arguing for a broader and more relational approach to the exploration of gender identities and gender issues in schools and classrooms. In order to avoid some of the regressive and counter-productive strategies associated with discourses about the 'underachieving boy', an exploration of some key principles and perspectives on social justice would be helpful.

What do we mean by 'social justice'?

As with the term 'gender', the concept of 'social justice' means different things to different people – and it refers to an inevitably complex tension between respect for difference and commitment to equality (Griffiths: 2003).

Distributive theories of social justice, associated with the ideas of John Rawls, stress the basic criteria of protection and promotion of maximal liberty for individuals, without infringing the liberty of others, and a commitment to fairness of distribution of social goods, adopting compensatory affirmative action measures to 'remove barriers arising from unequal power relations and preventing equity, access and participation' (Rawls: 1971: p60). Such a perspective focuses attention primarily on 'who gets what' within a liberal individualist framework. Much of the current concern about the 'underachieving boy' revolves around a narrow definition of 'equity' in terms of the distribution of the 'social' goods of academic credentials – rather than a broader concern with the social dimensions of gender relations.

A more empowering set of ideas is found in the work of Iris Marion Young (1990) who argues for a more relational definition of social justice, i.e. not only 'who gets what' but also 'how people treat each other in the process'. She proposes a framework that looks at 'actions, decisions about actions, and provision of the means to develop and exercise capabilities' (Young: 1990: 16) within which, 'Oppression and domination … should be the primary terms for conceptualising injustice' (pp8-9). Young defines five faces of oppression where 'the presence of any of these five conditions is sufficient for calling a group oppressed' (p64).

These five faces or dimensions are (pp 183-193):

- exploitation

- marginalization

- powerlessness

- cultural imperialism

- violence.

Using such dimensions to analyse and inform our practices, we can evaluate how far we are reproducing oppressive gender relations, and how far we are engendering social justice (Raphael Reed: 1998). Where learners are seen as a cypher for school success, one might call this exploitation, as we might also with the expectation that girls will help boys to be organized and on-task in the classroom. The invisibility and stigmatization of certain groups and individuals constitutes marginalization, as does the peripheralising of the emotional aspects of education in the pursuit of rationality. The lack of control that learners have over the curriculum, as well as the de-professionalisation of teachers in a culture of audit and accountability reinforces powerlessness. The use of white, male, middle-class values as established norms reflects cultural imperialism. Stress-inducing aspects of over-assessment, Assertive Discipline policies, child/adult bullying, racism, sexism and homophobia all reproduce conditions of violence.

Such ways of conceptualizing oppressive practices also allows us to recognize that individuals and groups may be both oppressed and oppressive to various degrees and at different times. This moves us away from labeling people as unacceptable, but rather encourages us to focus on people's behaviours and the impact of these behaviours on others.

Developing gender-fair strategies to counter the five faces of oppression requires the development of an inclusive participatory framework embracing staff, parents or carers and young people alike (Connell: 1993).

Such a framework entails:

Gender-fair Strategies for Engendering Social Justice	
Strategies to counter	Exemplars
Exploitation	• resisting attempts to distribute scarce resources by targeting them at learners who will bring greatest benefit to school reputation to the detriment of others • drawing attention to who is benefiting from the unpaid labour of others • encouraging responsibility for the consequences of one's own actions rather than attributing responsibility to others • challenging gendered employment practices where men may be over-represented in positions of power and privilege but women end up doing institutional housework..
Marginalisation	• ensuring that the interests of all groups and individuals are equally respected including those that are frequently invisible or stigmatised, for example gay and lesbian students and staff, or those with disabilities • valuing parents/carers as true partners in the process of education and engaging in respectful dialogues and activities between home and school • addressing the emotional dimensions of schooling as central rather than privileging solely the development of rationality, and developing learner self-esteem..
Powerlessness	• commitment by teachers and other adults to collaborative professional enquiry with a willingness to question taken-for-granted assumptions and an appreciation of the value of teachers' professional wisdom • listening to the voice of the learner, promoting consultation and self-evaluation and developing young people as researchers • empowering children to take control of their learning through effective learning strategies, negotiated curricula and aspects of personalised learning; making explicit and challenging gender dynamics that dis-empower and oppress others..

Strategies to counter	Exemplars
Cultural Imperialism	• promoting a culture of participatory and critical democracy with gender-fair active citizenship and international awareness • challenging racism, sexism and homophobia in all its forms and developing mutually respectful relationships that value difference • demonstrating a commitment to inclusion – changing the over-determining power of 'normative' beliefs and practices, and fully differentiating approaches to learning..
Violence	• resisting over-assessment and labelling of learners in terms of fixed abilities and learning styles • addressing issues of bullying in all of its forms through processes of restorative justice, conflict resolution and mediation • identifying and countering authoritarian management and pedagogic practices..

An approach based on the above framework is fully compatible with expectations enshrined in the Children Act 2004 (the legal underpinning for Every Child Matters: Change for Children - the programme aimed at transforming children's services) and the Youth Matters Green Paper published by the DfES in 2005. It also supports the development of an ethos that would enable schools to take part in the new UNICEF 'Rights Respecting Programme' and to gain the UNICEF Rights Respecting School Award – a nationwide scheme launched in 2006 and complementary to the Healthy Schools Award and Eco Schools recognition. (http://www.unicef.org.uk/tz/teacher_support/rrs_award.asp). Fundamental to the approach advocated in this book is the call to treat children as subjects and not objects, and to fully respect them and their human rights.

How to use this book

In the chapters that follow you will find practical ideas and resources to aid you as a learning community to explore these issues. The chapters are organised around the following five topics:

1. Relationship to Self: Identity Issues

2. Relationships with Others: Social Interactions

3. Learning and Teaching

4. Communication, Language and Literacies

5. Families, Communities and the Wider World.

Each chapter follows the same structure, with: a brief introduction, a set of ten age-appropriate activities (5-8 and 9-13) with reproducible stimulus material, guidance on further references and resources, and some suggestions for follow-up reflections and next steps. There is no expectation that you will use all of the material, or in any set order. Please feel free to take and adapt the ideas to suit your own circumstances. We would be very interested in receiving any feedback about how these ideas have been developed in practice to guide the ongoing development of this work in the future.

You will notice a number of recurrent themes throughout the book. The first is the importance of encouraging an inquiry-based approach to investigating the issues. This reflects our commitment to the continuing professional development of staff as critical 'reflective practitioners' (Ghaye and Ghaye: 2004) alongside engaging learners as co-enquirers in developing the learning environment and supporting self-evaluating schools (Macbeath et al: 2003a). At the heart of this process is the need to listen to children's voices – and to build learner agency and participation (Arnot et al: 2004; Kellet: 2005; Macbeath et al: 2003b; Rudduck and Flutter: 2004), moving beyond tokenistic attempts at pupil consultation (Fielding: 2004). This requires truly transformative dialogues – and the establishment of a context within which everyone feels safe to take some risks.

This latter point explains the second recurrent theme in the text: the centrality of developing emotional literacy and a sense of self-worth (Matthews: 2005). In our view, one of the most difficult aspects of developing mutual respect and gender-fair classrooms and schools are the defensive and resistant strategies used to avoid discussion of feelings or expressions of empathy. Such strategies themselves have a strong gender component, and affect adults and children alike. This has to change if we are to engender social justice in and through education.

Finally, a number of the suggested activities are not explicitly or singularly about gender per se – nor are they targeted differentially at boys and girls. This reflects our belief that gender issues are frequently embedded in wider cultural issues, including those associated with social class, disability and ethnicity, and that there are no immutable essential differences between girls and boys. Indeed, there are many common challenges shared by individual male and female learners as they struggle to develop their sense of a positive identity and their capability to participate ethically and democratically as active, global citizens in the complex and conflict-ridden world of today.

We hope that this book on engendering social justice goes some way towards supporting children in our schools in achieving these ends, and in creating healthy, inclusive and gender-fair learning environments for all.

References and further resources

Arnot, M. and Weiner, G. (eds) (1987) *Gender and the Politics of Schooling.* London: Unwin Hyman.

Arnot, M., David, M. and Weiner, G. (1999) *Closing the Gender Gap.* Cambridge: Polity Press.

Arnot, M., McIntyre, D., Pedder, D. and Reay, D. (2004) *Consultation in the Classroom: developing dialogue about teaching and learning.* Cambridge: Pearson.

Askew, S. and Ross, C. (1988) *Boys Don't Cry: Boys and Sexism in Education.* Buckingham: Open University Press.

Ashley, M. and Lee, J. (2003) *Women Teaching Boys: caring and working in the primary school.* Stoke on Trent: Trentham.

Ball, S.J., Maguire, M. and Macrae, S. (2000) *Choices, Pathways and Transitions Post-16: New youth, new economies in the global city.* London: RoutledgeFalmer.

Besag, V.E. (2006) *Understanding Girls' Friendships, Fights and Feuds.* Maidenhead: Open University Press.

Biddulph, S. (2003) *Raising Boys: Why Boys are Different – and How to help Them Become Happy and Well-balanced Men.* London: Thorsons.

Blair, M. and Holland, J. with Sheldon, S. (eds) *Identity and Diversity: gender and the experience of education.* Clevedon: Mulitlingual Matters and the Open University Press.

Bleach, K. (1998) *Raising Boys' Achievement in Schools.* Stoke on Trent: Trentham Books.

Bowles, R., Garcia Reyes, M. and Padiptyo, R. (2005) *Monitoring and Evaluating the Safer School Partnerships.* London: Youth Justice Board.

Browne, N. (1999) *Young Children's Literacy Development and the Role of Televisual Texts.* London: Falmer Press.

Browne, N. (2004) *Gender Equity in the Early Years.* Maidenhead: Open University Press.

Coffield, F. (2004) *Should we be using learning styles? What research has to say to practice.* Learning and Skills Research Centre: LSDA.

Cohen, M. (1998) 'A habit of healthy idleness': boys' underachievement in historical perspective' in Epstein, D., Elwood, J., Hey, V. and Maw, J. (eds) *Failing Boys? Issues in Gender and Achievement.* Buckingham: Open University Press.

Coleman, J. (2004) *Teenage Suicide and Self-Harm: a Training Pack for Professionals.* Brighton: Trust for the Study of Adolescence.

Connell, R.W. (1993) *Schools and Social Justice.* Toronto: Our Schools/Our Selves Education Foundation.

Connell, R.W. (1995) *Masculinities.* Cambridge: Polity Press.

Connolly, P. (1998) *Racism, Gender Identities and Young Children: social relations in a multi-ethnic, inner-city primary school.* London: Routledge.

Davies, B. (1989) *Frogs and Snails and Feminist Tales: Pre-school Children and Gender.* Sydney: Allen and Unwin.

Davies, B. (2003) 'Working with primary school children to deconstruct gender' in Skelton, C. and Francis, B. (eds) *Boys and Girls in the Primary Classroom.* Maidenhead: Open University Press.

DfES (2005) *Ethnicity and Education: The Evidence on Minority Ethnic Pupils.* DfES: Research Topic Paper RTP01-05.

Epstein, D. (ed) (1994) *Challenging Lesbian and Gay Inequalities in Education*. Buckingham: Open University Press.

Epstein, D., Elwood, J., Hey, V. and Maw, J. (eds) *Failing Boys? Issues in Gender and Achievement*. Buckingham: Open University Press.

Equalities Review (2006) *The Equalities Review*: Interim Report http://www.theequalitiesreview.org.uk Equal Opportunities Commission (2005) *Then and Now: 30 Years of the Sex Discrimination Act* http://www.eoc.org.uk.

Equal Opportunities Commission (2006) *Sex and Power: Who Runs Britain?* http://www.eoc.org.uk.

Fielding, M. (2004) 'Transformative approaches to student voice: theoretical underpinnings, recalcitrant realities' in *British Educational Research Journal* Vol 30, No 2, pp295-311.

Frater, G. (2000) *Securing Boys' Literacy*. London: Basic Skills Agency.

Francis, B. (2000) *Boys, Girls and Achievement: Addressing the Classroom Issues*. London: Routledge Falmer.

Francis, B., Skelton, C., Archer, L. (2002) *A systematic review of classroom strategies for reducing stereotypical gender constructions among girls and boys in mixed-sex UK primary schools* EPPI-Centre Review, version 1.1. London: EPPI-Centre, Social Science Research Unit, Institute of Education.

Frosch, S., Phoenix, A. and Pattman, R. (2002) *Young Masculinities*. Basingstoke: Palgrave.

Gardner, H. (1999) *Intelligence Reframed: Multiple Intelligences for the 21st Century*. New York: Basic Books.

Ghaye, A. and Ghaye, K. (2004) *Teaching and Learning Through Critical Reflective Practice*. London: David Fulton.

Gillborn, D. and Youdell, D. (2000) *Rationing Education: policy, practice, reform and equity*. Buckingham: Open University Press.

Gorard, S., Rees, G. and Salisbury, J. (2001) 'Investigating the pattern of differential achievement of boys and girls at school' in *British Educational Research Journal*, 27, pp125-139

Gray, J. (1992) *Men Are From Mars, Women Are From Venus*. New York: Harper Collins.

Griffiths, M. (2003) *Action for Social Justice in Education: Fairly different*. Maidenhead: Open University Press.

Gurian, M. (2001) *Boys and Girls Learn Differently: A Guide for Teachers and Parents*. San Francisco: Jossey-Bass.

Head, J. (1996) '*Gender Identity and Cognitive Style*' in Murphy, P.F. and Gipps, C.V. (eds) *Equity in the Classroom: Towards Effective Pedagogy for Girls and Boys*. London: Falmer Press

Hannan, G. (1999) *Improving Boys' Performance*. London: Folens.

Hart, S., Dixon, A., Drummond, M.J. and McIntyre, D. (2004) *Learning Without Limits*. Maidenhead: Open University Press.

Higher Education Funding Council (2005) *Young Participation in Higher Education*. HEFCE 2005/03.

Kellet, M. (2005) *How to Develop Children as Researchers: A Step-by-Step Guide to Teaching the Research Process*. London: Paul Chapman Publishing.

Kenway, J. and Willis, S. with Blackmore, J. and Rennie, L. (1998) *Answering Back: Girls, Boys and Feminism in School*. London: Routledge.

Jackson, C. (2006) *Lads and Ladettes in Schools*. Maidenhead: Open University Press.

Langley, J. (2005) *Boys Get Anorexia Too: Coping with Male Eating Disorders in the Family.* London: Lucky Duck Publishing/Paul Chapman Publishing.

Lloyd, B. and Duveen, G. (1992) *Gender Identities and Education.* Hemel Hempstead: Harvester Wheatsheaf.

Lloyd, G. (ed) (2005) *Problem Girls: Understanding and supporting troubled and troublesome girls and young women.* London: Routledge.

Lucey, H. (2001) 'Social class, gender and schooling' in Francis, B. and Skelton, C. (eds) *Investigating Gender: Contemporary Perspectives in Education.* Buckingham: Open University Press.

Lucey, H., Brown, M., Denvir, H., Askew, M. and Rhodes, V. (2003) 'Girls and Boys in the Primary Maths Classroom' in Skelton, C. and Francis, B. (eds) *Boys and Girls in the Primary Classroom.* Maidenhead: Open University Press.

Mac an Ghaill, M. (1994) *The Making of Men: Masculinities, sexualities and schooling.* Buckingham: Open University Press.

Macbeath, J. and Sugimine, H. with Sutherland, G. (2003a) *Self-evaluation in the Global Classroom.* London: RoutledgeFalmer.

Macbeath, J., Demetriou, H., Rudduck, J. and Myers, K. (2003b) *Consulting Pupils: A Toolkit for Teachers.* Cambridge: Pearson Publishing.

Mahoney, P. (1985) *Schools for the Boys: Co-education Reassessed.* London: Hutchinson.

Martino, W. and Pallotta-Chiarolli, M. (2003) *So What's a Boy? Addressing Issues of Masculinity and Schooling.* Maidenhead: Open University Press.

Matthews, B. (2005) *En.gaging Education: Developing Emotional Literacy, Equity and Co-education.* Maidenhead: Open University Press.

McNaughton, G. (2000) *Rethinking Gender in Early Childhood Education.* London: Paul Chapman.

Mirza, H. (1992) *Young, Female and Black.* London: Routledge.

Myers, K. (2000) *Whatever Happened to Equal Opportunities in Schools? Gender Equality Initiatives in Education.* Buckingham: Open University Press.

Noble, J., Brown, C. and Murphy, J. (2001) *How to Raise Boys' Achievement.* London: David Fulton.

O'Donnell, M. and Sharpe, S. (2000) *Uncertain Masculinities: Youth, Ethnicities and Class in Contemporary Britain.* London: Routledge.

OECD (2000) *Special Needs Education: Statistics and Indicators* Paris: Organisation for Economic Co-operation and Development: Centre for Educational Research and Innovation

OfSTED (2003a) *Yes he can – Schools where boys write well* (HMI 505) OfSTED Publications Centre.

OfSTED (2003b) *Boys' Achievement in Secondary Schools* (HMI 1659) OfSTED Publications Centre.

Osler, A. and Vincent, K. (2003) *Girls and Exclusion: Rethinking the agenda.* London: Routledge.

Paechter, C. (1998) *Educating the Other: Gender, Power and Schooling.* London: Falmer.

Parson, C., Godfrey, R., Annan, G., Cornwall, J., Dussart, M., Hepburn, S., Howlett, Wennerstrom, V. (2005) *Minority Ethnic Exclusions and the Race Relations (Amendment)* Act 2000 DfES Research Brief RB616.

Patterson, A. (2004) *Fit To Die: Men and Eating Disorders.* London: Lucky Duck Publishing/Paul Chapman Publishing.

Plummer, G. (2000) *Failing Working Class Girls.* Stoke on Trent: Trentham Books.

Raphael Reed, L. (1998a) 'Zero Tolerance, Gender Performance and School Failure' in Epstein, D. Elwood, J. Hey, V. and Maw, J. (eds) *Failing Boys? Issues in Gender and Achievement.* Buckingham: Open University Press.

Raphael Reed, L. (1998b) 'Power, pedagogy and persuasion: schooling masculinities in the secondary school classroom' in *Journal of Education Policy* Vol 13, No 4, pp501-517.

Raphael Reed, L. (1999) 'Troubling Boys and Disturbing Discourses on Masculinity and Schooling: a feminist exploration of current debates and interventions concerning boys in school' in *Gender and Education* Vol 11, No 1, pp93-110.

Rawls, J. (1971) *A Theory of Justice.* Cambridge MA: Belknap Press.

Reay, D. (2002) 'Shaun's Story: troubling discourses of white working class masculinities' in *Gender and Education* Vol 14, No 3, pp221-234.

Rotter, J. B. (1982) *The Development and Application of Social Learning Theory.* New York: Praeger.

Ruddock, J. and Flutter, J. (2004) *How to Improve Your School.* London: Continuum.

Salisbury, J. and Jackson, D. (1996) *Challenging Macho Values: Practical Ways of Working with Adolescent Boys.* London: Falmer Press.

Sewell, T. (1997) *Black Masculinities and Schooling: How Black Boys Survive Modern Schooling.* Stoke on Trent: Trentham Books.

Shibley Hyde, S. (2005) 'The Gender Similarities Hypothesis' in *American Psychologist* Vol 60, No 6, pp581-592.

Skelton, C. and Francis, B. (2003) *Boys and Girls in the Primary Classroom.* Maidenhead: Open University Press.

Smith, A. (1998) *Accelerated Learning in Practice: Brain-based Methods for Accelerating Motivation and Achievement.* Stafford: Network Educational Press.

Spender, D. and Sarah, E. (eds) (1980) *Learning to Lose.* London: The Women's Press.

Thorne, B. (1993) *Gender Play: Girls and Boys in School.* New Brunswick NJ: Rutgers University Press.

Weiner, G. and Arnot, M. (eds) (1987) *Gender Under Scrutiny.* London: Unwin Hyman.

Walkerdine, V. (1983) 'It's only natural: rethinking child-centred pedagogy' in Warrington, M. and Younger, M. with Bearne, E. (2006) *Raising Boys' Achievement in Primary Schools.* Maidenhead: Open University Press.

Wolpe, and Donald, J. (eds) *Is There Anyone Here from Education?* London: Pluto Press.

Walkerdine, V. (1989) *Counting Girls Out.* London: Virago.

Walkerdine, V. and Lucey, H. (1989) *Democracy in the Kitchen.* London: Virago Press.

Walkerdine, V., Lucey, H. and Melody, J. (2001) *Growing Up Girl: Psychosocial Explorations of Gender and Class.* London: Macmillan.

Warwick, I., Chase, E. and Aggleton, P. with Saunders, S. (2004) *Homophobia, Sexual Orientation and Schools*: a Review and Implications for Action DfES Research Report RR594.

Wilson, G. for DfES/Dept of Health (2003) *Using the National Healthy School Standard to Raise Boys' Achievement.* Wetherby: Health Development Agency.

Women and Work Commission (2006) *Shaping a Fairer Future* Women and Equality Unit: (DTI) http://www.womenandequlaityunit.gov.uk. Wood D (1998 2nd Edition) *How Children Think and Learn.* Oxford: Blackwell.

Younger, M. and Warrington, M. with Gray, J., Rudduck, J., McLellan, R., Bearne, E., Kershner, R. and Bricheno, P. (2005a) *Raising Boys' Achievement.* DfES: Research Report RR626.

Younger, M. and Warrington, M. with McLellan, R. (2005b) *Raising Boys' Achievement in Secondary Schools: Issues, Dilemmas and Opportunities*. Maidenhead: Open University Press.

Chapter One

Relationship to 'Self': Identity Issues

Introduction

Central to this chapter is the notion that all pupils and adults within the school community have the right to be respected and to have their self-esteem nurtured and promoted. The activities in this chapter consequently initially focus on the notions of 'Self', 'self-concept' and 'self-esteem'. There is also an emphasis on promoting equality and co-operation between all involved in the learning process. The pupils are asked to identify key qualities that they like about themselves and those that they may wish to develop and change in the future. Alongside this, they are asked to consider the significance or otherwise of stereotypes, including gender stereotypes, and the way in which certain people within our communities are represented in this manner, either in the media or within a classroom context. The idea that everyone has the right and need to participate in the learning process and should be empowered to do so is central to this set of activities.

How to use the activities

Note - For all ages, and especially for the younger age group, reading support might be needed. Where written responses are suggested, consider verbal feedback and circle time processes as alternatives.

Activity 1 - This is Me! Facts and Figures

In this activity pupils are asked to identify key aspects of their appearance alongside their specific likes and dislikes. They are also asked to identify key feelings and this is something that becomes a feature of many of the resources in the next five chapters, i.e. the promotion of pupils' emotional vocabulary and overall levels of emotional literacy. It may be helpful for the facilitator to have taken digital photographs of the pupils prior to the start of the session so that they can use these with the worksheets.

The worksheet for 5-8 year olds requires the pupils to record less information. Reception aged pupils can simply draw themselves and then tell the teacher five things about themselves. Responses can also be recorded by drawing into the shapes surrounding the portrait.

Activity 2 - Check it Out!

In this activity pupils are presented with a series of fact cards. These include such statements as: has black hair, loves to draw, likes snow, wears jewellery, was born in July, etc. The idea here is for pupils to move around the group that they are working in, asking others whether or not they fulfil the criteria detailed on the cards. They can then ask each individual to sign the card that applies to them and this process continues until everyone in the group has signed as many cards as possible. The aim here is to encourage pupils to co-operate and engage with each other in a very positive manner, accepting and celebrating difference. This activity should also help to break down pupil perceptions that girls and boys are diametrically different – but rather build awareness of similarities.

The 5-8 year group are asked to match the statement cards that apply to them. These include a child who likes drawing, watching television and making models. The pupils can sign or make a mark on the reverse of those cards they think apply to them. Reception aged pupils can be given the card that applies to them and the teacher can talk through why they match the pupil on the card.

Activity 3 – Dice Compliments

In this activity pupils are divided into groups of five and required to sit in a circle. Each of the pupils is numbered 1 to 5 and then required to throw the dice in turn. When the dice have been thrown, the pupil who has thrown the dice must then say something positive to the person who has been allocated that number, i.e. pay a compliment. This continues around the circle. The rules for this game are clearly indicated on the activity sheet. Once again, the aim here is to promote social behaviours, positive interactions between girls and boys and also to reinforce the fact that paying compliments is a very positive means of reinforcing each other's self-esteem. However, it needs to be made quite clear that compliments should be genuine and meaningful if they are to have this positive effect. This activity is the same for both age groups.

Activity 4 – My Ideal Self

In this activity pupils are asked to identify who they would like to be in the future and what they would like to do. The activity draws upon personal construct psychology. Pupils are asked to consider their ideal self and to draw and label their characteristics on the worksheet provided. They are then asked to stop and think of three things that they could do in order to move further towards such an ideal, i.e. setting targets. They are finally asked to share their thoughts with a partner. This activity is intended to reinforce self-esteem and to also promote the notion that change is entirely possible and having a positive attitude and being motivated are key features in moving forwards and developing oneself. The activity encourages pupils to gain a sense of 'agency' and control over their lives.

It may be more appropriate for Reception aged children to simply draw their 'best person' and to talk through why they would want to be like this person with their teacher.

Activity 5 – Keeping Healthy

In this activity pupils are asked to consider a range of options which may or may not promote good health, e.g. smoking, sleeping for eight hours a night, eating five vegetables a day, taking drugs, etc. This activity is intended to promote debate and conversation and further reinforce social skills and positive relationships. There is also the notion that everyone is entitled to have his or her own opinion and that opinions will differ. Rather than becoming distressed at such differences, we need to find a way to value them, to listen to each other, respect each other's opinions and views – but also be able to challenge each other's ideas in a respectful way.

It may be more appropriate for the teacher to lead this activity with the Reception aged children and to discuss each option in turn with the group. The cards can be sequenced on the whiteboard.

Activity 6 – How Would You Feel If...

In this activity pupils are presented during Circle Time with a range of statements depicting other pupils or individuals who may or may not have specific difficulties or complex needs. For example, one statement displays a boy in a wheelchair watching the football match at the side of the pitch i.e. being left out. Another picture depicts an old man looking from behind his curtains as three youths throw stones at his window, smashing one of them. The pupils are asked to consider how they would feel if they were in this situation and why this situation might engender such feelings. They are then asked to compare their ideas and discuss their interpretations during Circle Time. It will be necessary to have discussed Circle Time rules and ensure that all pupils are aware of the process prior to beginning this activity. The idea here is to promote empathy, i.e. pupils' ability to put themselves in others' shoes and consider others' feelings and the results of behaviours upon others. This also allows exploration of peer group gender behaviours that can be exclusive or destructive.

The activity is the same for the 5-8 year old group and a circle approach is used to elicit the pupils' views. It may be helpful for the teacher to model responses initially for the Reception aged children, for example, 'If I was this person I would feel…'

Activity 7 – Brainstorms

In this activity pupils are asked to consider what makes them feel good about themselves and how they can make others feel good, alongside what makes them feel negative and how they make others feel negative. They are then asked to consider similarities and differences between what they do and how they make others feel and to compare their responses with someone of the opposite sex. The aim here is to show both genders that behaviours may have the same impact regardless of who is behaving in that particular way, e.g. if a boy or a girl is aggressive or rude to someone, then that person will probably be affected in a very similar way.

The activity for the 5-8 year old group requires the pupils to draw their feelings. They are asked to draw what they look like when they feel good, how and when they make others feel good and what they look like and when they and others feel upset. They are then asked to compare their responses with someone of the opposite sex. It may be helpful to present these as four separate activities to the Reception aged pupils so as to avoid confusion and for the pupils to feedback their ideas as part of a circle discussion.

Activity 8 – Pupil Questionnaire – Action Research

In this activity the pupils are asked to interview a range of pupils in order to elicit their views as to what is positive and negative about their school. The aim is to empower pupils, enabling them to understand how they can play a key and pivotal role in making changes within the school environment. It will be necessary to ensure that pupils have the opportunities to feed the results that they gather back to staff in the school via the school council or another appropriate forum. They can also then make recommendations as to how the school can be made a happier and healthier place than currently is the case. This is the first instance in which pupils are asked to develop themselves as 'researchers'. The idea here is to empower them, providing a forum for hearing their voice and for dealing with issues of change within the school environment.

The activity is the same for the 5-8 year old group but the questions have been simplified. It may be more appropriate for the teacher to elicit the views of the Reception aged pupils via a whole class discussion in which responses are recorded by the teacher on a white board.

Activity 9 – Staff Questionnaire – Action Research

In this questionnaire the staff are asked the same questions as were asked of the pupils. The aim is to reinforce the fact that what goes on in school is a shared responsibility between staff and pupils and that pupils are in a key position to ensure that staff also feel happy, safe and able to do their jobs effectively. Once again, it's important that pupils have time and a forum in which to feed back the results that they gain from this activity. It may be helpful to allocate one key member of staff who can also feed back this information to a staff meeting for further discussion and development. It would also be a very positive outcome if pupils and staff were able to work together comparing their results from these two questionnaires and working in partnership in order to set specific targets which would and could make a positive impact on the school culture.

The activity is the same for both age groups. However, it may be more appropriate for Reception aged pupils to be allocated one question each to ask each staff member and responses could be taped rather than written down.

Activity 10 - Photo Shoot

In this final activity of the chapter, a selection of photographs or representations of people from the media are presented to pupils. For example - David Beckham, Naomi Campbell, Jade Jagger, Sol Campbell, Beyonce, etc. These will have been preselected and prepared by the facilitator. Once again a Circle Time approach is used and the pupils are asked to examine each image in turn, focusing on what actually makes this person 'beautiful' or 'attractive'. The aim here is not to specifically define notions of beauty but to question how these images are presented and the effect that they may have on other people who may not share these so-called beautiful attributes. The pupils are asked to consider whether this is a positive or negative thing and to consider, in particular, how such images may make people who do not look 'beautiful' by these definitions feel and how this impacts on their self-esteem and level of confidence and their ability to interact positively in the social context. This activity also facilitates discussion of who controls the images we see and the gender stereotypes contained within them.

The activity is the same for the 5-8 year old group but the questions have been simplified.

Practical strategies

Ten A4 activity sheets for 5-8 year olds:

Activity 1   – This is Me! Facts and Figures

Activity 2   – Check it Out!

Activity 3   – Dice Compliments

Activity 4   – My Ideal Self

Activity 5   – Being Healthy

Activity 6   – How Would You Feel If?

Activity 7   – Brainstorms

Activity 8   – Pupil Questionnaire – Action Research

Activity 9   – Staff Quiz – Action Research

Activity 10 – Photo Shoot!

Ten A4 activity sheets for 9-13 year olds:

Activity 1   – This is me! Facts and Figures

Activity 2   – Check it Out!

Activity 3   – Dice Compliments

Activity 4   – My 'Best' Person

Activity 5   – Keeping Healthy

Activity 6   – How Would You Feel if?

Activity 7   – Brainstorms

Activity 8   – Pupil questionnaire – Action Research

Activity 9   – Staff questionnaire – Action Research

Activity 10 – Photo Shoot

Further reference and resources

Davies, G. (ed) (1999) *Six Years of Circle Time – A Curriculum for Key Stages 1 & 2.* Bristol: Lucky Duck Publishing.

Dogra, N. Parkin, A. Gale, F. and Franke, C. (2002) *A Multidisciplinary Handbook of Child and Adolescent Mental Health for Front Line Professionals.* London & Philadelphia: Jessica Kingsley Publishers.

Lindenfield, G. (1995) *Self-esteem, Developing Self-worth, Healing Emotional Wounds.* London: Thorsons.

Moore, C. and Rae, T. (2000) *Positive People – a Self-esteem Building Course for Young Children.* Bristol: Lucky Duck Publishing.

Rae, T. (2000) *Confidence, Assertiveness, Self-esteem – a series of 12 sessions for Secondary School Students.* Bristol: Lucky Duck Publishing.

Stanley, N. and Manthorpe, J. (2002) *Students' Mental Health Needs, Problems and Responses.* London & Philadelphia: Jessica Kingsley Publishers.

Trentham Books, Westview House, 743 London Road, Stoke on Trent ST4 5NP Excellent range of professional development books for teachers on issues including equality, social justice and disability.

Warden, D. & Christie, D. (1997) *Teaching Social Behaviour – Classroom Activities to Foster Children's Interpersonal Awareness.* London: David Fulton Publishers.

Reflection and next steps

- It may be helpful to focus further on how staff within the school context can promote the self-esteem of all pupils, both within and outside of the taught curriculum. Given the importance of this work, it will probably be most appropriate for staff to allocate time to developing a whole school policy and approach to ensuring the development of and maintaining the self-esteem of pupils within the school. How to ensure this without reinforcing gender differentials but in a socially just and inclusive way is vital.

- Staff can also consider how they support each other in terms of reinforcing and building their own levels of self-esteem and confidence and consider the need to set up peer support systems within the school.

- Further work on promoting both physical and mental wellbeing could be conducted with a particular focus on dispelling any myths around mental ill health. Pupils need to be made aware of the fact that at least one in five of them will experience some form of mental ill health at some point in their lives and the fact that if they do have good self-esteem and are emotionally literate, they are less likely to suffer long term from such difficulties and more likely to recover quickly if they do encounter such difficulties.

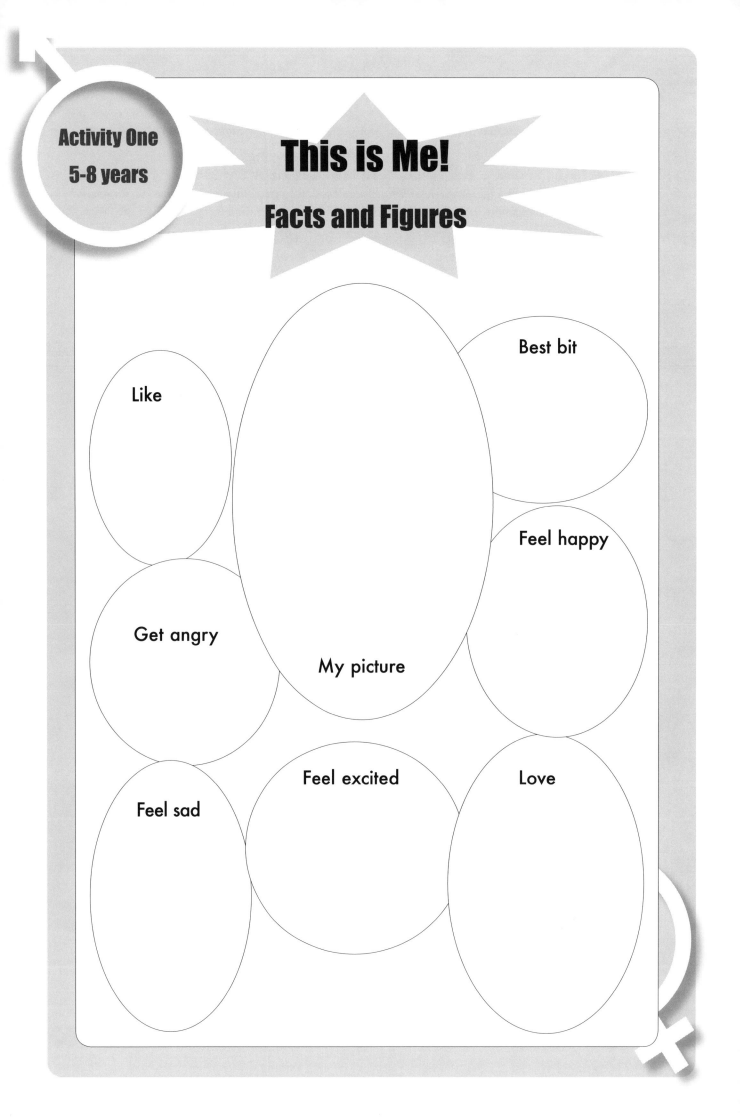

Activity One
5-8 years

This is Me!
Facts and Figures

Like

Best bit

Feel happy

Get angry

My picture

Feel sad

Feel excited

Love

Check it Out!

Discuss the scenarios below. Find at least one person in the group who 'matches' the child in the description. They can sign the back of the card. Keep going until everyone in the group has signed as many cards as possible.

Hates football	Likes to read	Loves swimming
Likes to watch cartoons	Is good at writing	Has a birthday in September
Can play a musical instrument	Has black hair	Has brown eyes
Has an XBox	Has a dog	Loves to draw
Was born in July	Has a sister	Is good at basketball

Dice Compliments

- You need five people in your group.
- Sit in a circle and number each person 1-5 around the circle.
- Ask one person to begin by throwing the dice. They then must say something positive to the person who has been allocated that number, such as:

I like the way you ....

I think you do .... well

I feel good about you because ....

- The next person in the circle then has a throw and pays a compliment.
- If someone throws a 6, then everyone has to pay him or her a compliment!

Enjoy the game!

My 'Best' Person

This is who and what I would like to be:

Draw and label

Stop, think, reflect. Think of three things you could do or change about yourself now in order to become your 'best' person. Share your thoughts with a partner.

Keeping Healthy

Cut out these statements and sort them into order – from the MOST to the LEAST healthy options

Feeling good about yourself	Sleeping for 8 hours a night	Eating junk food
Smoking	Relaxing	Drinking alcohol
Liking other people	Feeling happy	Taking exercise
Taking drugs	Eating 5 portions of fruit and vegetables a day	Not smoking
Feeling positive	Eating sweets	Eating at regular times
Having a holiday	Having good friends	Having lots of money
Feeling confident	Eating low-fat food	Not getting anxious about things

Take time to discuss these statements in your group. Can you agree?

Feed back your ratings to the rest of the group and compare your responses.

How Would You Feel If...?

Read the following scenarios and try to think how you would feel in each situation:

Disabled boy in wheelchair at side of football pitch watching the game.

Smallish black girl being threatened by white gang trying to take her money.

Only white boy in an all black class.

Two children standing by grave of a parent.

Boy looking in the mirror and picking his spots.

Girl not being allowed to join in the football match with the boys.

Girl at party left at side of room while others are dancing. She is very overweight.

Child listening at door whilst parents shouting in the next room.

Old man looking from behind his curtains as three youths throw stones.

Circle Time – sit as for Circle Time and finish the sentences: 'If I was in this situation I would feel .... because . ... '.

Compare your ideas and discuss your interpretations.

Brainstorms

(a)

I feel good when...........

I feel upset when.............

(b)

I make others feel good when..........

I make others feel upset when.........

Stop, think and reflect:

• Are there similarities and differences between columns (a) and (b)? What are they?

• Compare your responses with someone of the opposite sex. Are there similarities and differences? What are they?

Pupil Questionnaire
Action Research

1. What makes you feel happy in school?

   ....

2. What do you like doing the most?

   ....

3. Do teachers listen to you?

   ....

4. Do teachers like the pupils?

   ....

5. What makes you feel sad in school?

   ....

6. What do you not like doing?

   ....

7. What could you do to make your school a better place?

   ....

8. What could the grown-ups do to make your school a better place?

   ....

   ....

   ....

Thank you for contributing to our research.

Staff Questionnaire

Action Research

1. What makes you feel happy in school?

   ....

2. What activities do you enjoy most?

   ....

3. Do you think that the pupils in school listen to the adults' views?

   ....

4. Do you feel that the pupils in the school show respect to and like the staff?

   ....

5. What makes you feel sad in school?

   ....

6. What activities do you dislike the most?

   ....

7. What could you do to make the school a happy and healthy place?

   ....

8. What would you like the pupils' to do in order to make the school a happy and healthy place?

   ....

   ....

   ....

Thank you for contributing to our research

Photo Shoot

Select a series of photos of people from the media, for example, David Beckham, Jade Jagger and Beyonce.
In a Circle Time session, examine each image in turn, focusing on the following questions:

• Is this a 'beautiful' person?

• Why? What makes them beautiful?

• Do other people want to look like them? If so, why?

• If someone doesn't look like this and sees this picture, how will they feel?

• Do we see other kinds of people on the TV or in newspapers and magazines?

This is Me!
Facts and Figures

I like ....
....
....

I love ....
....
....

I feel angry when
....
....

My favourite
hobby is ....
....

My Portrait

The music I like is
....
....

My height is ....
....
....

My hair colour is
....
....

My best subject
is ....
....

I get worried
about ....
....

I don't like.......
....
....

Check it Out!

Complete the fact file by talking to everyone in the group. Find at least one person who meets the criteria for a fact card.

That person should sign the card. Keep going until everyone in the group has signed as many cards as possible.

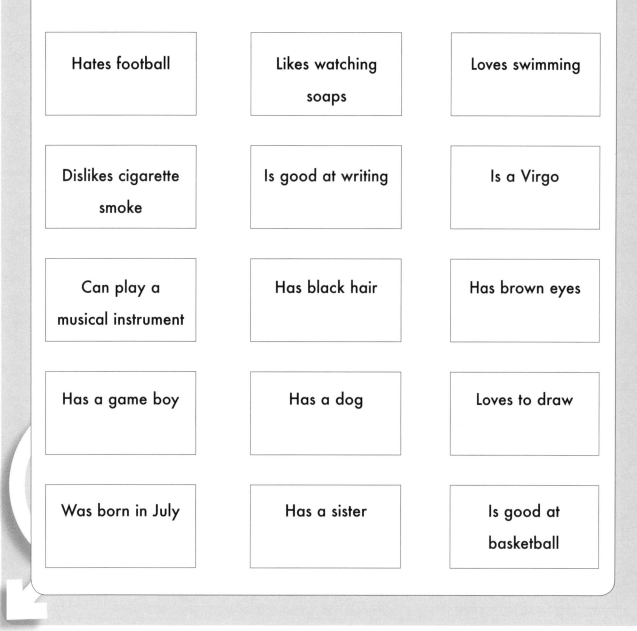

Hates football	Likes watching soaps	Loves swimming
Dislikes cigarette smoke	Is good at writing	Is a Virgo
Can play a musical instrument	Has black hair	Has brown eyes
Has a game boy	Has a dog	Loves to draw
Was born in July	Has a sister	Is good at basketball

Dice Compliments

- You need five people in your group.
- Sit in a circle and number each person 1-5 around the circle.
- Ask one person to begin by throwing the dice. They then must say something positive to the person who has been allocated that number, for example:

I like the way you ....

I think you do .... well.

I feel good about you because ....

- The next person in the circle then has a throw and pays a compliment
- If someone throws a 6, then everyone has to pay him or her a compliment!

Enjoy the game!

My Ideal Self

How would you like to be? What would you like to do? What is your 'Ideal Self'? Draw and label your characteristics in the thought bubbles.

My Ideal Self

Stop, think, reflect. Think of three things you could do or change about yourself now in order to move closer to your ideal. Share your thoughts with a partner.

Keeping Healthy

Cut out these statements and sort them into order – from the MOST to the LEAST healthy options.

Feeling good about yourself	Sleeping for 8 hours a night	Eating junk food
Smoking	Relaxing	Drinking alcohol
Liking other people	Feeling happy	Taking exercise
Taking drugs	Eating 5 portions of fruit and vegetables a day	Not smoking
Feeling positive	Eating sweets	Eating at regular times
Having a holiday	Having good friends	Having lots of money
Feeling confident	Eating low-fat food	Not getting anxious about things

Take time to discuss these statements in your group. Can you agree? Feed back your ratings to the rest of the group and compare your responses.

How Would You Feel If...?

Read the following scenarios and try to think how you would feel in each situation:

Disabled boy in wheelchair at side of football pitch watching the game.

Small black girl being threatened by white gang trying to take her money.

Only white boy in an all black class.

Two children standing by grave of a parent.

Boy looking in the mirror and picking his spots.

Girl not being allowed to join in the football match with the boys.

Girl at party left at side of room while others are dancing. She is very overweight.

Child listening at door whilst parents shouting in the next room.

Old man looking from behind his curtains as three youths throw stones at his house.

Circle Time – sit as for Circle Time and finish the sentences: 'If I was in this situation I would feel .... because ....'. Compare your ideas and discuss your interpretations.

Brainstorms!

(a)

What makes me feel good about myself?

(b)

How do I make others feel good?

(a)

What makes me feel negative about myself?

(b)

How do I make others feel negative?

Stop, think and reflect:

- Are there similarities and differences between (a) and (b)? What are they?

- Compare your responses with someone of the opposite sex. Are there similarities and differences? What are they?

Pupil Questionnaire

Action Research

1. What makes you feel happy in school?

   ....

2. What activities do you enjoy most?

   ....

3. Do you feel that the adults in school listen to the pupils' views?

   ....

4. Do you feel that the adults in the school show respect to and like the pupils?

   ....

5. What makes you feel sad in school?

   ....

6. What activities do you dislike the most?

   ....

7. What could you do to make the school a happy and healthy place?

   ....

8. What would you like the adults to do in order to make the school a happy and healthy place?

   ....

   ....

   ....

Thank you for contributing to our research.

Staff Questionnaire
Action Research

1. What makes you feel happy in school?

   ....

2. What activities do you enjoy most?

   ....

3. Do you think that the pupils in school listen to the adults' views?

   ....

4. Do you feel that the pupils' in the school show respect to and like the staff?

   ....

5. What makes you feel sad in school?

   ....

6. What activities do you dislike the most?

   ....

7. What could you do to make the school a happy and healthy place?

   ....

8. What would you like the pupils' to do in order to make the school a happy and healthy place?

   ....

   ....

   ....

Thank you for contributing to our research.

Photo Shoot!

Select a series of photos of people from the media, for example, David Beckham, Jade Jagger, Beyonce.

In a Circle Time session, examine each image in turn, focusing on the following questions:

- What makes this person beautiful or attractive?
- How, where and when have they been photographed?
- Who decides who is and isn't a beautiful person?
- Do you think other people want to look like or be like this? If so, why and is this a positive or negative thing?
- How do you think these images make people who do not look like this feel?
- Would it be a good thing if we saw all sorts of people represented in the media as apposed to just the 'beautiful' few?
- How else might people be described as 'beautiful'?

Chapter Two

Relationships with Others: Social Interactions

Introduction

This chapter explores the central importance for girls and boys of positive and supportive relationships with others. The initial focus is on the nature of friendship and the ways in which people can behave both positively and negatively in their relationships with each other. The pupils are asked to focus particularly on the ways in which they communicate with each other and how learning to be a good listener is a vital aspect of communication and helps to maintain positive relationships. Pupils are asked to consider ways in which they can help each other in the problem-solving process and to identify people who can help them and support them to sort out the kinds of problems and difficulties that they meet in their relationships and daily lives. There is also a focus on eliminating bullying within the school context, specifically that of the playground, in order to create a safe, happy, inclusive and bully-free environment. The ways in which pupils themselves can contribute towards such a goal is also central to this chapter and the notion of self-efficacy is again reinforced, i.e. that pupils can take control and can be empowered by the systems within the school to participate more effectively, having their say and contributing to positive changes and outcomes for all involved.

How to use the activities

Note - For all ages, and especially for the younger age group, reading support might be needed. Where written responses are suggested, consider verbal feedback and Circle Time processes as alternatives.

Activity 1 - My World

In this activity pupils are required to draw a diagram to show who makes up their world. They can include people who help them, people who support them, those who help them to learn and those who are good friends to them etc.

The activity for the 5-8 year old group is entitled 'People Who Help Me In My World' and requires the pupils to draw all the people who help them. Reception aged pupils may wish to talk through their drawings with their teacher so that they can then be labelled appropriately.

Activity 2 - Brainstorm Activity

In this activity pupils are asked to consider, 'Who Is A Good Friend' – what do they do and what do they not do? The aim is to highlight the positive aspects of friendship and the way in which pupils can support each other, show empathy and co-operate in order to encourage and allow for the development of both social and emotional skills and educational achievement. It's very important that pupils understand the importance of emotional support and the ways in which emotional difficulties can prevent effective learning from taking place. It is also important to highlight the fact that the rules for friendship and the definitions of friendship will be no different for adults, i.e. staff members in the school context would also need to be able to identify these qualities and promote them in each other if they are to work together as a truly effective and productive team. This activity can also promote awareness of the similarities between girls and boys of their friendship needs and qualities.

The activity for the 5-8 year old group is presented as a page of statements. Pupils are asked to identify those who are being good friends and those who are not acting in a friendly manner. They are also required to discuss why they have made these judgements.

Activity 3 – Listen Up Actions

In this activity pupils are presented with a range of secret direction cards. They are asked to act out a conversation in pairs – one person taking the lead and the other apparently listening. The person who is asked to take on the latter role is provided with the card. The card gives the direction as to what they are supposed to do whilst the other person is talking or vice versa. For example, 'talk to the person and give them good eye contact', or, 'talk to the person but copy all their movements'. The aim here is for the pupils to act out their short conversations to the rest of the group so that the inappropriate social behaviours can be identified. It is also important for pupils to question and identify how these inappropriate social behaviours made them feel if or when they were the recipients of them. It may be helpful for the facilitator to also participate in these activities, pointing out how difficult it is not to get upset, hurt or angry when people do not respond to you in a pro-social manner. Pupils can also be encouraged to then identify what they can do in order to address such behaviours. This activity can be done in mixed-gender and same-gender pairs.

This activity is the same for both age groups. However, it may be more appropriate for the teacher to whisper each of the 'secret directions' to reception aged pupils who may not be able to read the directions on the cards. It may also be appropriate to simplify some of the directions.

Activity 4 – Good Listening

In this activity pupils are asked to consider and identify how they feel when they are listened to and how they feel when they are not listened to. It is suggested this activity be undertaken by both adults and pupils. Once again, it will be interesting to point out the similarities, i.e. the feelings that teachers experience when they are not listened to will not be very different to the feelings experienced by pupils when they find themselves in the same position. There is also a focus here on the kind of non-verbal behaviours that we would observe in a 'good listener'. This is very important as it encourages pupils to be a bit more analytical in their observations and to begin to self-reflect on their own behaviours when engaged in social interactions with others.

The 5-8 year old group are asked to draw and label two pictures. The first picture is of a good listener and the second is of a bad listener. They are then asked to identify how they feel when they are listened to and how they feel when they are not listened to. Reception aged pupils can do the second part of the activity via discussion with their teacher.

Activity 5 – Guess Who?

In this activity a collection of pictures will have been made of famous footballers, pop stars, TV, personalities, etc. Each of the pupils (and the facilitator) can have one of these pictures sticky-taped to their backs. However, they are not allowed to see this picture. The pupils in the group are then asked to walk around the room and to question others and answer others' questions about these characters without naming them in order to be able to identify who their famous person is. This practical activity encourages pupils to practise their listening and communication skills. They are also asked to co-operate and work together in order to complete this task successfully.

The activity is the same for the 5-8 year old group but the famous people have been substituted with people who help us. The pictures are taped onto pupil's backs and the same process is followed as for the older pupils.

Activity 6 – Who Would You Be?

In this activity pupils are asked to choose two famous people – one that they'd really like to be and one that they wouldn't want to be so much. They are then asked to clarify why they would choose to be one person as opposed to the other and to consider whether or not others would make the same choices as they would. The idea here is to show that we all have personal preferences that are different and need to be respected. Where children select atypical 'role models' by gender, any attempt by their peers to question or challenge this can provide a useful prompt for a further discussion of how stereotypes close down opportunities and the right to choice.

The 5-8 year old group are required to draw a famous person that they would like to be and then one that they wouldn't like to be. They then answer the same questions as the older pupils. For Reception aged pupils, this can be done in discussion with the teacher if appropriate.

Activity 7 – Problem Cards

The pupils are presented with six problem cards which all concern pupils who are being bullied, either by peers, parents or teachers. They are usually being bullied because they have a specific difficulty, for example, cleft palate, cerebral palsy, learning difficulties or (in one instance) because they are Black. The aim here is to highlight the notion of difference, including disabilities, special educational needs, ethnicities and gender. If a school context is to be truly inclusive, then the pupils need to be able to not only empathise with others but also truly value and respect differences between them.

The activity is the same for the 5-8 year old group but the problems have been adapted so as to be more relevant to this age group. For the younger pupils, it may also be more appropriate for the teacher to present each problem in turn and ask for the pupils' responses as part of a Circle Time discussion.

Activity 8 – Our Playground

In this activity the pupils are asked to develop a questionnaire in order to find out what pupils think they need in order to have a safe, happy, inclusive and bully-free environment in the playground. The pupils are asked to devise a questionnaire, which will elicit the views of pupils, staff and parents/carers. The aim of this activity is to reinforce the fact that the safety of pupils in schools is a shared responsibility. As with previous questionnaires, it will be necessary to ensure that pupils have a forum in which to feed back their findings and that the findings themselves do lead to specific targets being set which will engender positive changes for all involved. There is a particular focus here on promoting the pupil's ability to monitor behaviour and avoid bullying within the playground and there is also a focus on gender aspects of the use of space, for example, how to ensure equal access to ball games, or to use of the central areas.

The activity for the 5-8 year old group is entitled 'Our Playground'. The pupils are presented with a series of statements about a range of activities and apparatus for the playground. The pupils are asked to tick against those that they feel would make their playground a safer and happier place. They are also required to contribute three of their own ideas. For Reception aged pupils it may be more appropriate for the teacher to enlarge the activity sheet to A3 size and to elicit the pupils' views and ideas via a whole class discussion.

Activity 9 – My Best Playground

This activity leads directly on from Activity 8 in that the pupils are asked to design the kind of playground they think people really want in order to feel safe, happy, included and bully-free. The pupils are presented with a 'blank' playground in which they can design their own safe place to play, giving reasons for and labelling the kinds of choices and decisions that they've made on the plan.

The activity is the same for the 5-8 year old group but is titled 'My Best Playground'. Pupils are asked to label their design. Alternatively, the younger pupils can talk through their ideas with the teacher.

Activity 10 – Circle Spin

In this activity, the facilitator spins a bottle on the carpet in the middle of the circle where pupils are seated as for Circle Time. The bottle will stop at various points around the circle and point to different individuals who are then asked to either ask the question or complete the sentence completion task. This activity focuses on bullying and asks the pupils to consider why they think people become bullies in the first place. The idea here not to demonise bullies but rather to engender understanding and to begin to put in place some preventative measures so as to avoid these kinds of situations from occurring in the first place.

The activity is the same for the 5-8 year old group although the questions have been simplified.

Practical strategies

Ten A4 activity sheets for 5-8 year olds:

Activity 1   – People Who Help Me In My World

Activity 2   – Who Is A Good Friend?

Activity 3   – Listen Up! Secret Direction Cards

Activity 4   – Good Listening

Activity 5   – Who Are You?

Activity 6   – Who Would You Be?

Activity 7   – Problems!

Activity 8   – Playground Preferences

Activity 9   – My Best Playground

Activity 10 – Circle Spin and sentence completion tasks – questions for Circle Time

Ten A4 activity sheets for 9-13 year olds:

Activity 1   – My World

Activity 2   – Who Is A Good Friend?

Activity 3   – Listen Up - Actions

Activity 4   – Good Listening

Activity 5   – Guess Who?

Activity 6   – Who Would You Be?

Activity 7   – Problem Cards

Activity 8 – Our Playground

Activity 9   – A Blank Sheet

Activity 10 – Circle Spin

Further references and resources

Boulger, D. (2002) *Building on Social Skills.* Staffs NASEN.

DfES (2000) *Bullying – Don't Suffer in Silence: an anti-bullying pack for schools.* DfES 0064/2000.

Epstein, D. (ed) (1994) *Challenging Lesbian and Gay Inequalities in Education.* Buckingham: Open University Press.

Goldthorpe, M. (1998) *Poems for Circle Time and Literacy Hour.* Cambridge: LDA.

Jackson, N. Jackson, A. and Monroe, C. (1983) *Skill Lessons and Activities, Getting Along with Others, Teaching Social Effectiveness to Children.* Illinois: Research Press.

Mosley, J. (1996) *Quality Circle Time in the Primary Classroom.* Cambridge: LDA.

Robinson, G. Sleigh, J. & Maines, B. (1991) *No Bullying Starts Today - Awareness Raising Days on Bullying.* Bristol: Lucky Duck Publishing.

Weare, K. (2000) P*romoting Mental, Emotional and Social Health – A Whole School Approach.* London: Routledge.

Willesden Bookshop, Willesden Green Library, 95 The High Road, London NW10 4QU – A wide range of children's books with many specialist collections of dual language, multi-cultural titles as well as a good range of books challenging sexual stereotypes.

Reflection and next steps

- It may be helpful to consider conducting an anti-bullying initiative. This event could be designed for either a single year group within the school context (Year 6/7) or perhaps be designed to include all year groups. A useful resource in planning such a day is *No Bullying Starts Today* by Robinson, Sleigh and Maines (1991). The aims of such a day would include the following:

  - to promote understanding that bullying happens

  - to promote understanding that bullying is damaging to the person who receives it

  - to understand that bullies are not nasty people and may not be fully aware of how their behaviour damages other people

  - to extend the definition of bullying to a wider range of behaviours

  - to learn something about group processes

  - to experience group work

  - to provide opportunity through creative work for young people to express feelings about bullying

  - to provide empowering opportunities for problem solving. What can we do? What will we do?

  - to celebrate the work done on the day

  - to prepare for further work to be done in the future.

- It may also be helpful to further raise awareness as to the nature and consequences of bullying by accessing relevant video resources, for example Brown, Robinson, and Maines (1993) *Broken Toy* Bristol: Lucky Duck Publishing (video) Central Television's video entitled *Sticks and Stones* and Maines and Robinson (1992) *Michael's Story – the No Blame Approach* Bristol: Lucky Duck Publishing (video).

- Staff could also consider how bullying is recorded and monitored within the school and how efficient the systems currently are. How are racist incidents and homophobic incidents reported? What is the process for addressing these particular kinds of bullying and who is engaged in contributing to policy in this area, e.g. parents and different religious and ethnic groups?

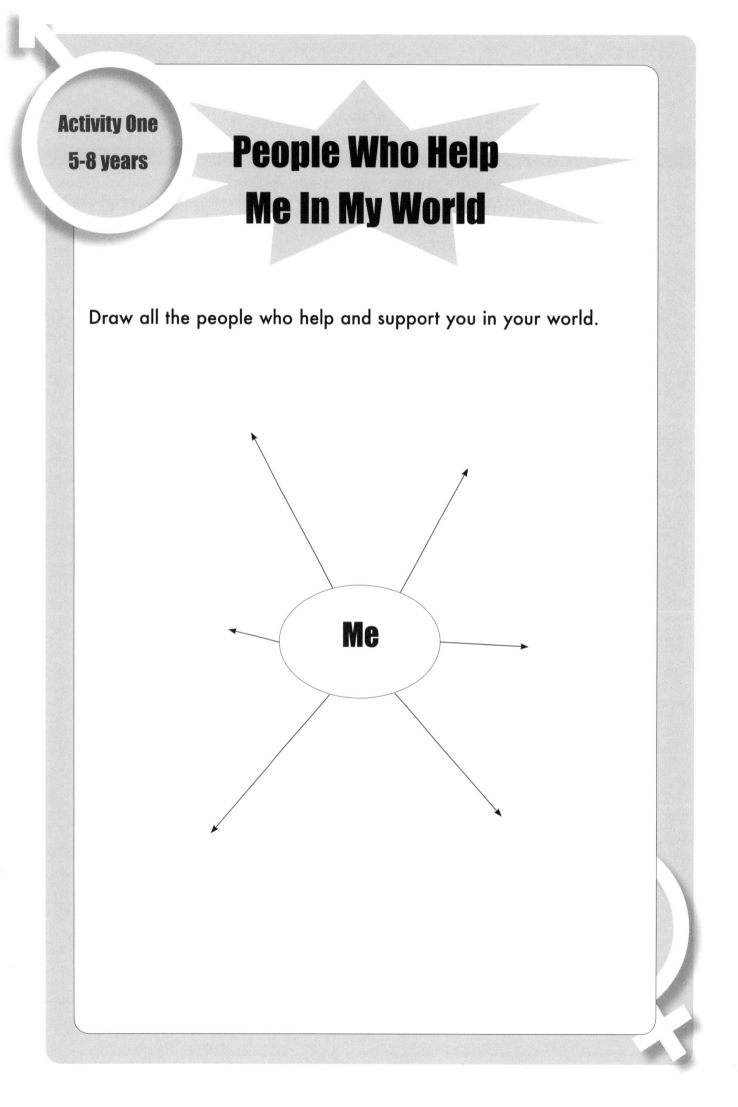

People Who Help Me In My World

Draw all the people who help and support you in your world.

Me

Who Is A Good Friend?

**Activity Two
5-8 years**

One child helping another who is hurt ○

One child stealing another's mobile phone ○

Two children whispering about another child near to them ○

One child copying her friend's work in a test ○

One child 'teaching' another to read ○

One child sharing his sweets ○

One child sitting watching others laughing ○

One child fouling another in football match ○

One child sharing his computer game ○

One child helping another to learn a game ○

One child putting plaster on another's knee ○

One child pulling another's hair ○

Discuss in your group. Why is each person either a good or not so good friend?

Listen Up!

Secret Actions

Talk to the person but don't look at them	Talk to the person and smile at them and look interested
Talk to the person but yawn and scratch your head a lot	Talk to the person and give them good eye contact
Talk to the person but copy all their movements	Talk to the person and nod your head to encourage them
Talk to the person but keep looking at your watch or the clock	Talk to the person and lean forward when they speak
Talk to the person but turn your body away from them	Talk to the person and move your chair nearer to them when they speak
Talk to the person but look blank and stare at them	Listen to the person but don't say a word

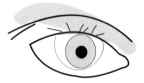 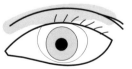

Good Listening

A good listener

A bad listener

When I am listened to I feel...

....

When I am not listened to I feel...

....

Guess Who?

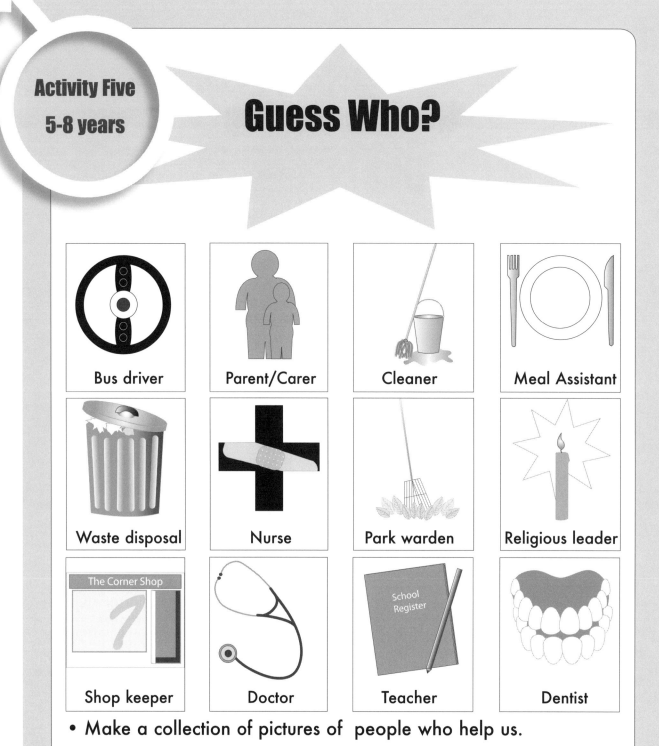

Bus driver | Parent/Carer | Cleaner | Meal Assistant

Waste disposal | Nurse | Park warden | Religious leader

Shop keeper | Doctor | Teacher | Dentist

- Make a collection of pictures of people who help us.
- Each pupil has a picture sticky-taped to their backs. They do NOT see the picture.
- Pupils then walk around the room and question others and answer others' questions about these people.
- Eventually, each pupil should be able to 'name' their person.
- Practising listening skills should help pupils complete the task successfully.

Who Would You Like to Be?

(a)

A famous person
I would like to be:

(b)

A famous person
I wouldn't like to be:

- Why did you choose to be person (a)?

  ....

  ....

- Why did you not choose to be person (b)?

  ....

  ....

- Do you think other people would make the same choice as you?
  Check it out!

  ....

  ....

- If you could be person (a), how would this make your life better?

  ....

  ....

Problem Cards

My best friend has gone off with a new boy. He doesn't want to play with me at break any more and I am on my own all the time. I feel lonely. What can I do?

My dad wont let my best friend come to our house to play. He says he won't have black people in our house. What can I do?

I am in Year 1 and I am scared of my new teacher. I liked my old teacher in Reception better because she didn't shout. What can I do?

My best friend can't read or write properly yet. She just finds it too hard. She is getting upset because we have our SAT tests this year and she is worried about them already. How can I help her?

Five boys in year 2 keep bullying me. They call me 'fat cow' and other horrible names because I'm big. I don't want to go to school any more. What can I do?

My mum tells me to fight back if people bully me but when I do that I get into trouble at school. What can I do?

Our Playground

What would you like? Tick against the statement if it is something you feel would make your playground a safe and happy place:

Quiet area ◯

Indoor games area ◯

Bully box ◯

Buddies working with younger or more vulnerable children ◯

Teacher(s) supervising games ◯

Disabled access ◯

Boys and girls playing football ◯

Toy library ◯

Garden ◯

Skipping ◯

Swimming pool ◯

TV or computer room access ◯

Your choice .... ◯

Your choice .... ◯

My Best Playground

Draw and label your own playground:

Circle Spin

Complete the following statements:

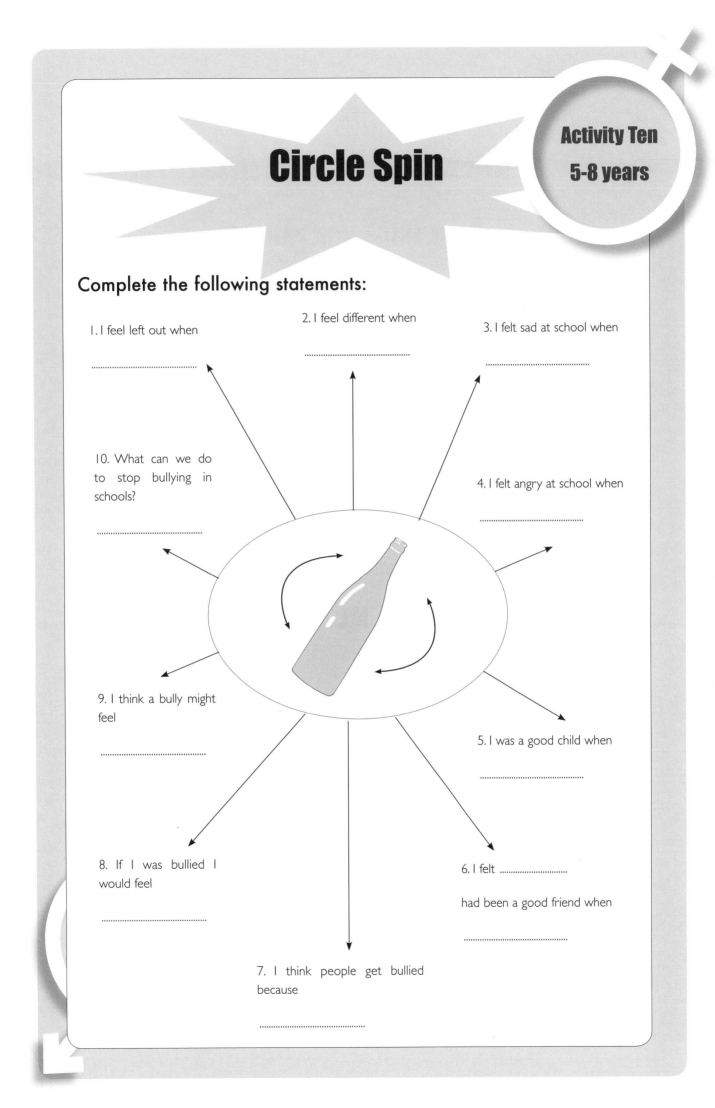

1. I feel left out when

....

2. I feel different when

....

3. I felt sad at school when

....

10. What can we do to stop bullying in schools?

....

4. I felt angry at school when

....

9. I think a bully might feel

....

5. I was a good child when

....

8. If I was bullied I would feel

....

6. I felt ....

had been a good friend when

....

7. I think people get bullied because

....

My World

Stop, think and reflect

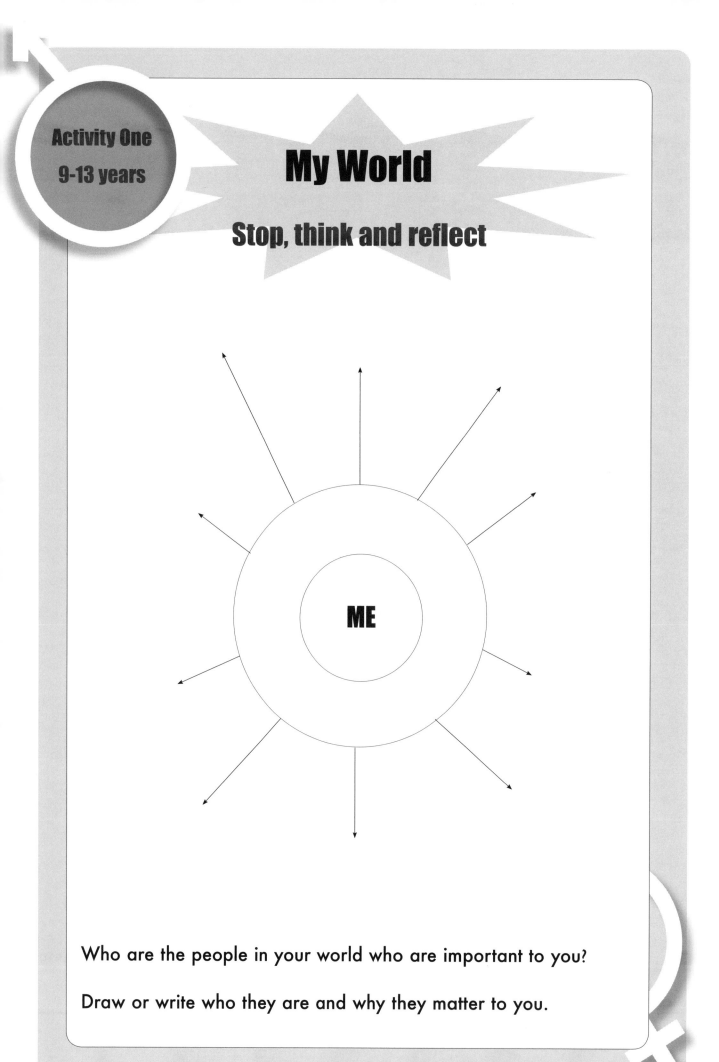

ME

Who are the people in your world who are important to you?

Draw or write who they are and why they matter to you.

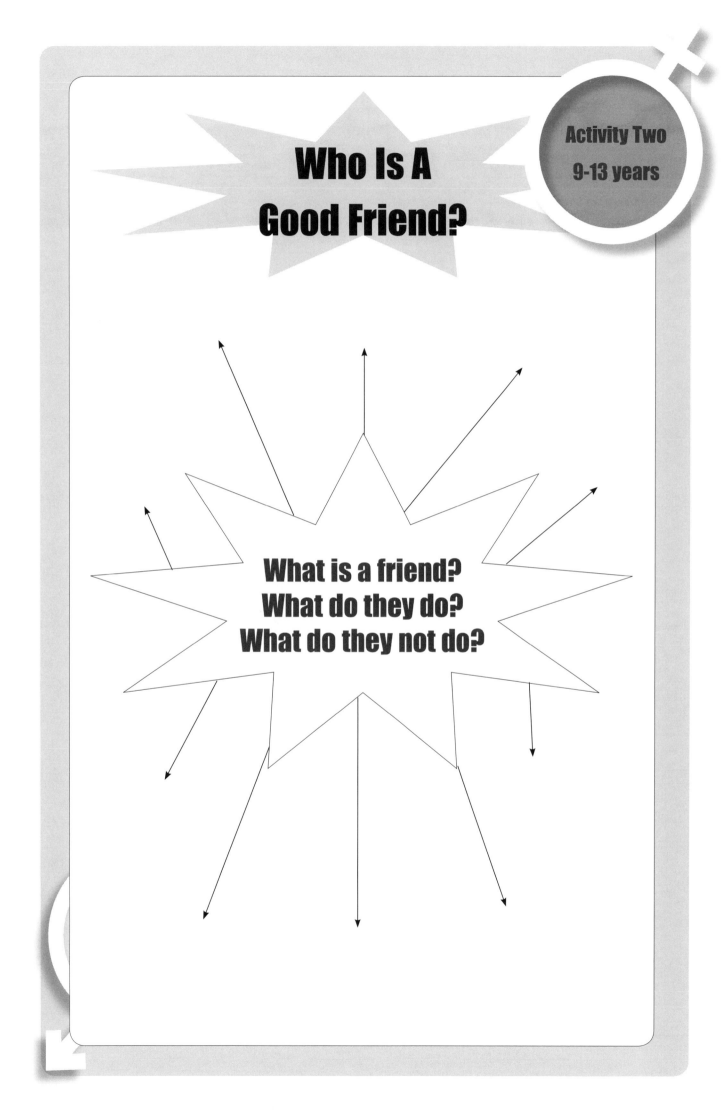

Who Is A Good Friend?

Activity Two
9-13 years

What is a friend?
What do they do?
What do they not do?

Listen Up!

Secret Direction Cards

Talk to the person but don't look at them	Talk to the person and smile at them and look interested
Talk to the person but yawn and scratch your head a lot	Talk to the person and give them good eye contact
Talk to the person but copy all their movements	Talk to the person and nod your head to encourage them
Talk to the person but keep looking at your watch or the clock	Talk to the person and lean forward when they speak
Talk to the person but turn your body away from them	Talk to the person and move your chair nearer to them when they speak
Talk to the person but look blank and stare at them	Listen to the person but don't say a word

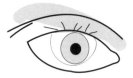

Good Listening

How do we feel?

(a) When we are listened to?

....

(b) When we are not listened to?

....

Stop, think and reflect:

What non-verbal behaviours would you observe in a GOOD LISTENER? Use the sub-headings to help prompt your thinking.

1. Voice ....

2. Eye contact ....

3. Spatial distance ....

4. Fiddling movements ....

5. Positive ....

6. Head movements ....

7. Facial expression ....

8. Gestures ....

Who Are You?

Practising listening skills!

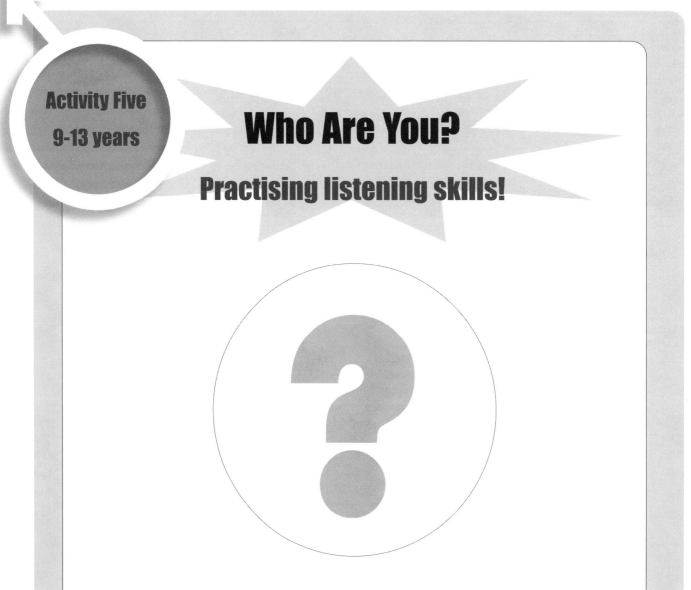

- Make a collection of pictures of people who help us.

- Each pupil has a picture sticky-taped to their backs.
  They do NOT see the picture.

- Pupils then walk around the room and question others and
  answer others questions about these people.

- Eventually, each pupil should be able to 'name' their person.

- Practising listening skills should help pupils complete the
  task successfully!

Who Would You Like To Be?

Choose two famous people – one who you would really like to be and one who you wouldn't.

(a) I would like to be:

Name ....

Gender ....

Ethnicity ....

Hair colour............................

Eye colour ....

Likes / Dislikes.......................

....

Talents ....

....

Friends.................................

....

(b) I wouldn't like to be:

Name ....

Gender ....

Ethnicity ....

Hair colour............................

Eye colour ....

Likes / Dislikes.......................

....

Talents ....

....

Friends.................................

....

- Why did you choose to be person (a)?

- Why did you not choose to be person (b)?

- Do you think other people would make the same choice as you? Check it out!

- If you could be person (a), how would this make your life better?

Problems!

Problem Cards

My best friend has got a cleft palatte. She is really brave and had lots of operations. one girl in our class just hates her though and calls her 'freakface'. She even says she hopes my friend will die during her next operation next month. She's just evil and I need to know how to stop her. Please help.

My teacher is really nice but she is a bit too soft. four of the older kids in the school keep on shouting at her and saying she's a dog because she's spotty and skinny. I want to help. What can I do?

I am in Year 7 and I hate my new school. The boys in my class bully me because I am fat and useless at football. What can I do?

I have got cerebral palsy and it means I have to use crutches and can't walk very well. Some of the other girls in my class keep trying to trip me up and call me spastic. They say I'll never get a boyfriend. What can I do?

My step-dad says I'm thick because I can't spell. He's always making me feel stupid in front of the rest of the family. I hate him. He's a bully. What can I do?

Most of the people in my class are white and they are okay – but two of the girls keep calling me monkey face because I am African. What can I do?

Playground Preferences

'Creating a safe, happy, inclusive and bully-free environment'

- Create a questionnaire to find out what people think they need in order to have a safe, happy, inclusive and bully-free environment.
- Ask pupils, staff and parents (If you can!)
- Use the headings and ideas below to help you formulate your questions.
- Pilot your quiz in the group.
- Try it out and then feedback your information.

Key headings and ideas

- How and when do they feel safe, happy and secure?
- Can both sexes access football?
- Use of space – different areas.
- Do you need to have football or other ball games every day?
- Games and activities – which are good and why?
- Monitoring behaviour.
- Is everyone included?
- Avoiding bullying.
- How are pupils and staff with disabilities included?
- Use of pupils and staff to monitor behaviour.

My Best Playground

Design the playground you think people really want in order to be safe, happy and bully-free. Label and give reasons for your choices and decisions.

My playground

Circle Spin

Complete the following sentences.

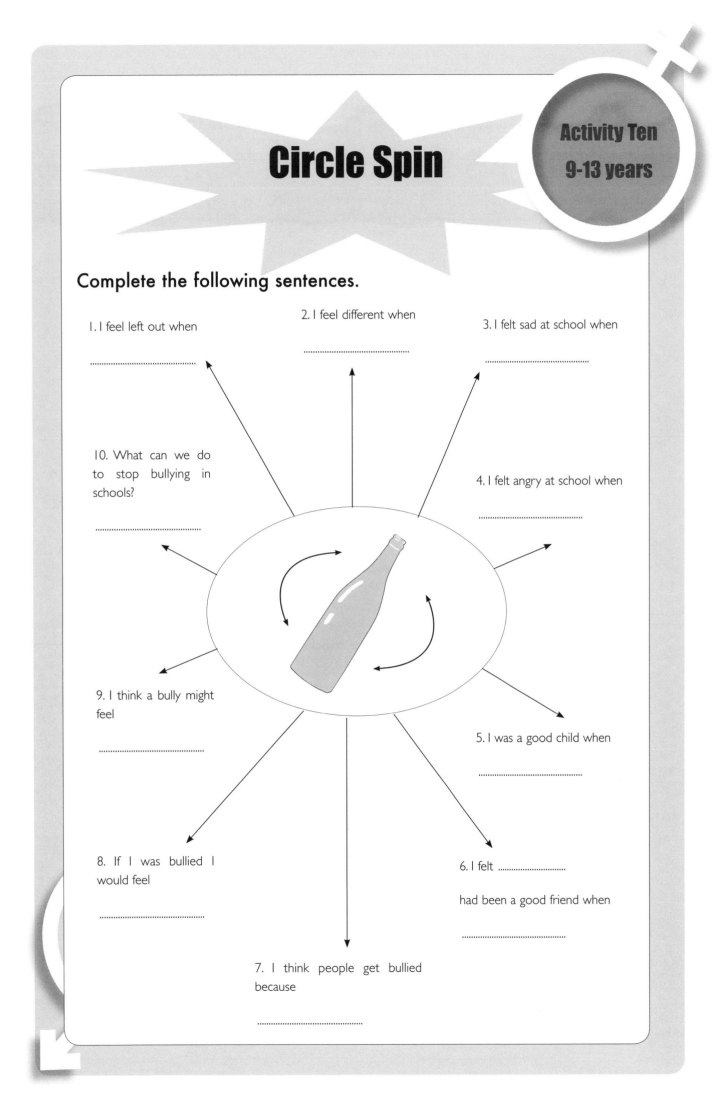

1. I feel left out when

....

2. I feel different when

....

3. I felt sad at school when

....

10. What can we do to stop bullying in schools?

....

4. I felt angry at school when

....

9. I think a bully might feel

....

5. I was a good child when

....

8. If I was bullied I would feel

....

6. I felt ....

had been a good friend when

....

7. I think people get bullied because

....

Chapter Three

Learning and Teaching

Introduction

In this chapter the focus is primarily upon developing a range of learning and teaching styles and strategies within the school context. There is also a focus on the need for teachers and pupils to be democratic in the ways in which they share responsibility for ensuring that effective learning can take place in their school and classrooms. Pupils are also asked to consider the different ways in which they learn and to identify their own learning styles and needs and the ways in which these may or may not be being addressed within the current context.

A particular focus is given to promoting equality within the classroom, i.e. who talks and how and when they are asked or provided with opportunities to talk. Pupils are asked to consider how much talking is done by teachers, as opposed to pupils, and how much interaction there is between boys and their teachers and girls and their teachers. There is also a focus on pupils becoming more self-aware and self-reflective as to their own readiness to engage in the learning process and staff are required to reflect upon the ways in which they ensure that both genders have equal access to all learning activities within the classroom context. The notion of accessibility is central to this chapter and the importance of staff ensuring that the curriculum is accessible to all pupils regardless of gender, class, ethnicity, ability or disability is stressed.

How to use the activities

Note - For all ages, and especially for the younger age group, reading support might be needed. Where written responses are suggested, consider verbal feedback and circle time processes as alternatives.

Activity 1 - My Ideal Teacher

In this activity pupils are asked to identify the skills and qualities of their 'ideal' teacher. The idea here is to highlight the key aspects and behaviours that the pupils know promote their learning, reinforce their self-esteem and ensure that they can become confident, independent learners. It may be helpful for the facilitator to also complete this activity alongside the pupils and to share their responses and ideas with them.

The activity for the 5-8 year old group is similar but called 'The Best Teacher In The World.' Pupils are asked to draw and then label their picture of the best teacher. Reception aged pupils can simply complete the drawing and then discuss their ideas with their teacher.

Activity 2 - The Perfect Pupil

The activity directly follows on from Activity 1 and is essentially the reverse side of the coin, i.e. the pupils now have to identify the qualities that they would see in a 'perfect' pupil. Once again, it would be helpful for the facilitator to also participate in this activity. The aim here is to reinforce the fact that behaviour and learning within the classroom context should be an essentially democratic process with the pupils and the staff being equally accountable and responsible for making sure that learning can take place. Initially the pupils may feel that behaviour in the classroom, for example, is the direct responsibility of the teacher. However, once both of these activities have been completed it may become more apparent that in fact they also have a responsibility to be well-behaved, to listen when necessary, to be attentive and to show respect for the teacher and their peers just as the it is the teacher's responsibility to ensure that the lesson is engaging, that pupils can access what's going on and that pupils feel respected, nurtured and listened to. It's a two-way process and it's very important that this kind of respect is shared between both the pupils and staff and that there is a shared understanding of responsibilities and fairness within the classroom context.

The activity for the 5-8 year old group is similar but called 'The Best Pupil In The World.' Pupils are asked to draw and then label their picture of the best pupil and to answer a series of questions. Reception aged pupils can simply complete the drawing and then discuss their ideas with their teacher.

Activity 3 – How Do You Like To Learn?

In this activity pupils are prompted to consider the different ways in which people like to learn. Pupils are asked to identify their own learning styles and the lessons that best suit these styles. This information can be extremely useful in terms of feeding back to staff. It may help in terms of planning lessons that are truly inclusive and incorporate a range of teaching strategies and ideas so as to ensure that all pupils, regardless of learning style, can effectively participate. When pupils are asked how other lessons could be made better for them, it is suggested that this kind of information must be fed back to staff so that they can be empowered to provide a more inclusive learning context. It is important however to stress in this activity that one's 'learning style' is not a fixed commodity; we might have preferences but these can and do change over time, or shift according to context.

The activity for the 5-8 year old group asks the pupils to identify the ways they like to learn by circling the statements that apply to them. It may, however, be more appropriate for the teacher to talk through each example individually with the younger pupils.

Activity 4 – Who Talks? (1) An Investigation

In this activity pupils are asked to consider access to 'talk' within their classroom by undertaking two timed observations. They are asked to identify how much time within a ten minute period the teacher talks and how much time within a ten minute period the pupils talk. This will involve two pupils working simultaneously: one observing the teacher talking and the other observing the pupils talking within this period. The aim here is to identify if there is an appropriate balance. For example, the teacher who talks for 80% of this observed period may or may not be engaging the pupils in the classroom. However, the teacher who engages with pupils and encourages them to participate in dialogue may well have gained more attention and the learning may be more productive. A more sophisticated activity might focus on the type of talk and interaction that is taking place in the classroom, and how this facilitates or blocks engagement of some participants in the learning process.

The 5-8 year old group are required to observe how many times their teacher talks within a ten minute period and then how many times a pupil talks within the same amount of time. They are asked to make use of an egg timer and to record observations in a tally chart. For Reception aged pupils it may be more appropriate to use practical resources to keep a record of how often each person talks during a ten minute period. For example, placing marbles in a jar might provide a more meaningful visual image. It may also be necessary to reduce the observation time to three minutes.

Activity 5 – Who talks? (2) An Investigation

This investigation focuses on a different aspect of equality within the classroom. Pupils are asked to observe two lessons for a ten minute period and to identify how many times boys are chosen by teachers to answer questions or how many times boys make a verbal contribution and then to identify how many times girls are chosen by teachers to answer questions or how many times girls make a verbal contribution. Should the results show that boys tend to answer more questions or are asked to answer more questions then this will need to be explored further. Follow up discussion needs to consider actions that staff and pupils might take to make a difference. The idea here is to promote the notion that both genders should have equal access to the verbal aspects of learning and an equal opportunity to make such contributions within lessons.

The activity for the 5-8 year old group is entitled 'Boys and Girls Talking' and the pupils can once again use an egg timer to time their observations. They are asked to choose how many times the teacher chooses a girl to answer a question and then how many times a boy is chosen within the given time scale. They are then asked to identify who seems to be asked the most and to consider why this might be the case. For Reception aged pupils it may be more appropriate to use practical resources to keep a record of how often girls and boys are asked to answer the teacher's questions during a ten minute period. Once again, placing marbles in a jar might provide a more meaningful visual image. It may also be necessary to reduce the observation time to three minutes.

Activity 6 – Behaviour for Learning

In this brainstorming activity pupils are asked to identify how they know when they are ready for learning. The aim here is to reinforce the fact that we cannot learn when we feel emotionally distressed or we are preoccupied about something or we have just had an argument with a friend, etc. How pupils manifest their lack of preparedness to learn may be gendered – but the full range of behaviours that signal this need to be acknowledged. We need to be calm, seated appropriately (if suitable), focused and motivated. How pupils can ensure that they are in such a position could be an appropriate follow-on task here. For example, they may like to consider how pupils in their school are supported when they are in distress and when they do feel emotionally unable to cope. What happens in order to ensure that they can begin to calm down and then access the learning situation?

The activity is the same for the 5-8 year group but pupils are required to draw and label a picture to show when they are ready to do their work. Reception aged pupils can simply draw the picture and then discuss their ideas with the teacher.

Activity 7 – A Teachers' Quiz

This quiz is intended for teachers and asks them to engage in the process of reflection. They are asked to focus specifically on how equal their practice is and whether or not they ensure equal opportunities within the classroom and within their social interactions across staff and with pupils in the school. It is suggested that staff's responses here could be shared within the context of a staff meeting and that key difficulties or areas that need to develop further should be identified so as to begin to further promote equal opportunities within the school. This activity is the same for both age groups but it is anticipated that younger pupils will simply hand the questionnaire to relevant staff for completion whilst older pupils may wish to interview teachers and record their responses in note form or using a tape recorder.

Activity 8 – Assessment Stress

In this activity pupils are asked to consider how the assessment processes that need to take place in school now, e.g. SATS, GCSEs, etc., can be made less stressful for all of those concerned. The pupils are asked not only to consider their own strategies and ideas but to also ask friends and teachers for theirs. It is hoped that by engaging in this activity it should be possible to identify and begin to develop systems that help pupils and staff to manage stress in these situations more effectively.

The activity is differentiated for the 5-8 year group as the pupils are presented with a scenario involving another child who gets stressed whenever there is a test. The pupils are asked to identify what and who might help him. This can be completed via a circle discussion if pupils are unable to record their thoughts in writing.

Activity 9 - Plan your Ideal Lesson

This activity is intended for both teachers and pupils in order to encourage them to plan what they perceive to be a ideal lesson. They are asked to consider issues of inclusion, learning styles and how the classroom is set out and particularly how pupils are grouped for activities. The idea here is to reinforce the fact that what goes on in the classroom is a shared responsibility and that if pupils do not feedback to teachers how they best learn and what they would like to see happen in lessons, then it is not always possible for teachers to modify and change their practice. Communication needs to be effective and continuous.

Pupils in the 5-8 year old group are required to plan their ideal lesson and to include a start, middle and end to this session. This can be completed in three drawings and Reception aged pupils can also discuss their ideas with the teacher.

Activity 10 - How True Is This?

The final activity asks the pupils to read a statement to parents, pupils and members of staff in the school and to ascertain whether or not they agree with it. The statement basically proposes that a curriculum informed by the principles of equal opportunity will be essentially inclusive in that it will be accessible to all pupils regardless of gender, class, ethnicity, ability or disability. The idea is to ask the key stakeholders whether or not they agree with this statement and to then identify ways in which they think the curriculum can be made more inclusive within the school context. It will be important that this information is gathered together in a well-structured and logical manner so that it can be easily presented to management within the school. If there are areas that stakeholders identify as requiring further work or development, e.g. there is gender imbalance or there are is a problem in terms of including pupils with disabilities or those with special needs, then these need to be identified and clarified so that specific targets can be set in order to ensure improvements and appropriate changes.

The 5-8 year old group are presented with a series of statements that include a range of special needs and differences. The pupils are asked to tick or cross each statement with reference to the evaluation: Our school is a good place for all of these people. Reception aged pupils can discuss their ideas with the teacher on an individual basis or as part of a whole class circle discussion.

Practical strategies

Ten A4 activity sheets 5-8 year olds:

Activity 1   – The Best Teacher In The World

Activity 2   – The Best Pupil In The World

Activity 3   – I Like To Learn By

Activity 4   – Who Is Talking?

Activity 5   – Boys and Girls Talking

Activity 6   – I Am Ready To Do My Work

Activity 7   – A Teachers' Quiz

Activity 8   – Testing Times

Activity 9   – My Ideal Lesson

Activity 10 – How True Is This?

Ten A4 activity sheets for 9-13 year olds:

Activity 1   – My Ideal Teacher

Activity 2   – The Perfect Pupil

Activity 3   – How Do You Like to Learn?

Activity 4   – Who Talks? (1) An Investigation

Activity 5   – Who Talks? (2) An Investigation

Activity 6   – Behaviour For Learning

Activity 7   – A Teachers' Quiz

Activity 8   – Assessment Stress

Activity 9   – Plan Your Ideal Lesson

Activity 10 – How True Is This?

Further references and resources

Casey, J. (2002) *Getting it Right – A Behaviour Curriculum.* Bristol: Lucky Duck Publishing.

Caviglioli, O. and Harris, I. (2000) *Mapwise: Accelerated Learning Through Visible Thinking.* Stafford: Network Educational Press Ltd.

McConnou, S. (1990) *Interpersonal Communication – A Personal Skills Course for Young People.* Surrey: Nelson.

Millard, E. (1997) *Differently Literate: Boys, Girls and The Schooling of Literacy.* London: Falmer Press.

Mosley, J. and Sonnet, H. (2003) *101 Games for Social Skills.* Cambridge: LDA.

Murphy, P F. and Gipps, C V. (eds) (1996) *Equity in the Classroom: Towards Effective Pedagogy for Girls and Boys.* London: Falmer Press

Robinson, G. and Maines, B. (1998) *Circle Time Resources.* Bristol: Lucky Duck Publishing.

Torrington, D, and Weightman, J, (1993) 'The Culture and Ethos of the School' in Preedy, M. (ed) (1993) *Managing the Effective School.* London: Paul Chapman Publishing.

Wardle, C. and Rae, T. (2002) *School Survival – Helping Students Survive and Succeed in Secondary School.* Bristol: Lucky Duck Publishing.

Reflection and next steps

- It may be helpful for school staff to consider setting up stress management programmes in order to specifically support pupils with examination stress. These can be done prior to SATS or school-based exams and tests, as and when appropriate. It may be useful to consider accessing or utilising a programme such as *Strictly Stress – Effective Stress*

Management for High School Students (2001). This programme is designed to be used in the secondary phase with both groups of pupils and whole classes and is specifically aimed at pupils who appear to be experiencing unacceptable levels of stress in their lives and require support in order to understand, acknowledge and cope with specific stresses or sources of stress. These are the kinds of pupils who may exhibit low self-esteem and levels of confidence alongside difficulties in asserting themselves. However, pupils who are experiencing life changes such as death, divorce, change of school, etc., or who have specific difficulties in organising themselves and their workloads (particularly during exam periods) would also benefit from this programme. This has direct relevance to certain gendered avoidance behaviours and strategies that undermine pupil ability to learn effectively.

- It may also be helpful for staff to consider their own levels of stress and ways in which this can be alleviated and addressed within the school context.

- Staff may wish to further consider the ways in which they present the curriculum to pupils and the extent to which their learning and teaching strategies are inclusive. It may be helpful to arrange for additional training in order to utilise such methods as mind mapping or accelerated learning techniques. 'Accelerated learning attempts to connect to and build upon prior knowledge and understanding whilst presenting an overview of the learning challenge to come. Participants set positive outcomes and define targets towards each of these outcomes. Information is then presented in visual, auditory and kinaesthetic modes and is reinforced through different forms of intelligent response. Frequent, structured opportunities to demonstrate understanding and to rehearse for recall are the concluding feature of the cycle' (Smith, A. foreword in Caviglioli, O. and Harris, I.: 2000).

The Best Pupil In The World

Questions to answer:

What would he or she look like?

How would they behave in and out of class?

What would teachers feel and think about them?

What would pupils feel and think about them?

How would they work?

What would their relationships with others be like?

How would they feel about themselves?

Illustration of the 'model' pupil.

How Do You Like To Learn?

Circle the statements that apply to you:

I like writing on my own.

Picture of child doing a mixture of writing and practical tasks in a lesson.

I like copying down a fact and repeating it until it's 'known'.

I like talking through my ideas.

I like drawing facts and visualising them in my head.

I sometimes fidget because the teacher is going on for too long .

I like doing calculations on paper.

I like sorting out problem with apparatus such as cubes or counters.

I like working on my own.

I like listening to my teacher.

I like making a model or construction using my hands.

I like working in a group.

- Which is your favourite or best lesson? ....
- Why is this? ....
- How can other lessons be made better for you?

....

....

Who Talks?

You will need a stopwatch or an egg timer.

Time it! How many times does the teacher talk in ten minutes?

1	2	3	4	5	6	7	8	9	10

Tally

⊬⊬⊬

Time it! How many times does a pupil talk in ten minutes?

1	2	3	4	5	6	7	8	9	10

Tally

⊬⊬⊬

Who talks the most?

Boys and Girls Talking

Use a ten minute egg timer.

Observation (1)	Observation (2)
How many times does the teacher choose a girl to answer a question? Use Ticks ◯ TOTAL ◯	How many times does the teacher choose a boy to answer a question? Use Ticks ◯ TOTAL ◯

Talk about your findings in the group.

• Who gets asked the most questions?

....

• Why do you think this is the case?

....

• How can lessons become more equal?

....

....

Activity Six
5-8 years

Behaviour For Learning

I can work well when...

A Teachers Quiz

Ask your teachers to reflect upon the following questions

1. Are boys and girls listed alphabetically in the school registers?

2. What criteria do you use for lining up?

3. Are you aware of the forms of address you use e.g. head teacher, dinner lady, lollipop lady; different roles and responsibilities addressed differently e.g. nursery teacher (Mrs Smith) /nursery nurse (Jane)?

4. Do you make sure parents are welcome and that communications are accessible?

5. Do you encourage pupils to work in mixed gender groups for classroom activities?

6. Do you think single sex groupings are sometimes more appropriate and, if so, when and why?

7. Do you have strategies to deal with cycles of dominant behaviour?

8. Do ALL pupils have the opportunity to participate fully e.g. in discussion, practical sessions.

9. Do you ensure equal access to all activities for boys and girls e.g. computer, cooking, football, etc

10. Do you encourage boys to do their fair share of tidying up and girls to lift and carry?

11. Do you ensure that pupils do not sit in single sex groups in assembly?

12. How do you ensure that your reactions to poor behaviour are not influenced by preconceived expectations regarding gender, ethnicity and ability?

Thank you for your thinking time!

Assessment Stress

Peter doesn't like doing tests. He gets stressed. What will help him?
Who can help him? Draw and label your picture of Peter.

Think carefully: how can his friends help?

how can his teachers help?

how can he help himself?

Plan Your Ideal Lesson

Draw and label:

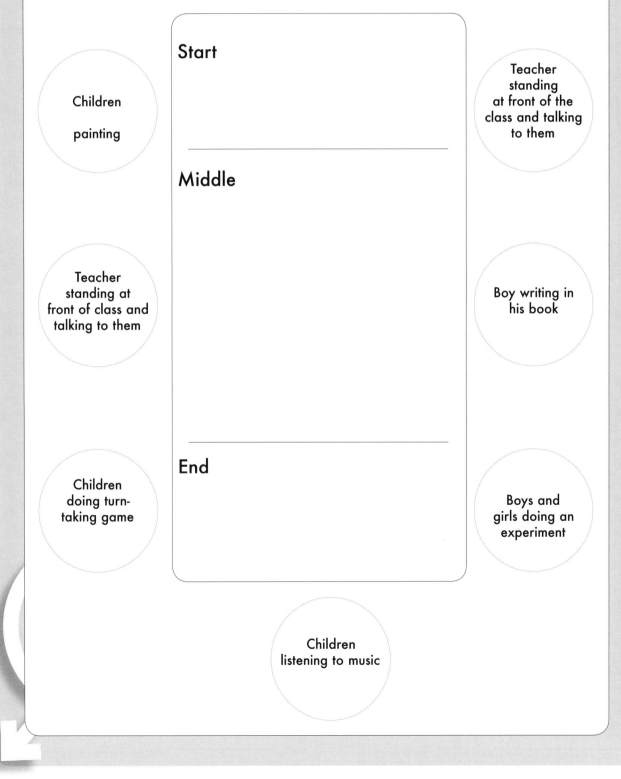

Start

Middle

End

Children painting

Teacher standing at front of the class and talking to them

Teacher standing at front of class and talking to them

Boy writing in his book

Children doing turn-taking game

Boys and girls doing an experiment

Children listening to music

How True Is This?

Our school is a good place for all of these people:
Tick against each sentence

Boy in poor looking clothes and malnourished   ◯

Girl with cleft palette   ◯

Boy finding the work difficult   ◯

Girl in posh clothes   ◯

Muslim girl   ◯

Somali boy   ◯

Girl singing on stage – a star!   ◯

Sikh boy   ◯

Deaf boy   ◯

Blind boy   ◯

Afro-Caribbean girl   ◯

Traveller child   ◯

Girl with cerebral palsy.   ◯

Child in wheelchair   ◯

Boy with facial disfigurement   ◯

Girl playing football   ◯

How can we make it a better place for these people?

My Ideal Teacher

What do they look like? What are their skills and qualities? What makes the ideal teacher?

The Perfect Pupil

Questions to answer:

What would he or she look like?

How would they behave in and out of class?

What would teachers feel and think about them?

What would pupils feel and think about them?

How would they work?

What would their relationships with others be like?

How would they feel about themselves?

Illustration of the 'model' pupil

How Do You Like To Learn?

Circle the statements that apply to you:

I like writing on my own

I like sharing ideas and understanding best when I can talk it through

I like learning by doing – especially using my hands

I remember facts best by drawing them out or visualising things in my head

I like to copy things down and repeat them until I know the facts

I like doing problems with apparatus e.g. building using cubes etc

I like doing calculations on paper

I like sorting out problema with apparatus, such as cubes or counters

I like working on my own

I like lessons that have a mixture of writing and practical tasks

I get fidgety when the teacher goes on for too long

I enjoy listening to the teacher talk

- Which is your favourite or best lesson?
- Why is this?
- How can other lessons be made better for you?

Who Talks (1)?

An Investigation

How 'equal' is your classroom.

Choose a lesson and do two timed observations.

1. How much time within a ten minute period does the teacher talk?

2. How much time within a ten minute period do the pupils talk?

Minutes	Teacher / Pupils		Minutes	Pupils / Teacher	
1			1		
2			2		
3			3		
4			4		
5			5		
6			6		
7			7		
8			8		
9			9		
10			10		

Who Talks (2)?

An Investigation

How 'equal' is your classroom?

Choose two lessons and do a ten minute observation in each.

(1) How many times boys are chosen to answer the teacher's questions/make a contribution and (2) How many times girls are chosen to answer the teacher's questions/make a contribution. (Use a tally system IIII)

Lesson I	Lesson 2
Date	Date
Teacher	Teacher
Time from to	Time from to

BOYS	BOYS
TOTAL	TOTAL
GIRLS	GIRLS
TOTAL	TOTAL

- Feedback your results to the rest of the group.
- Where are the differences and similarities?
- How can lessons become more 'equal'?

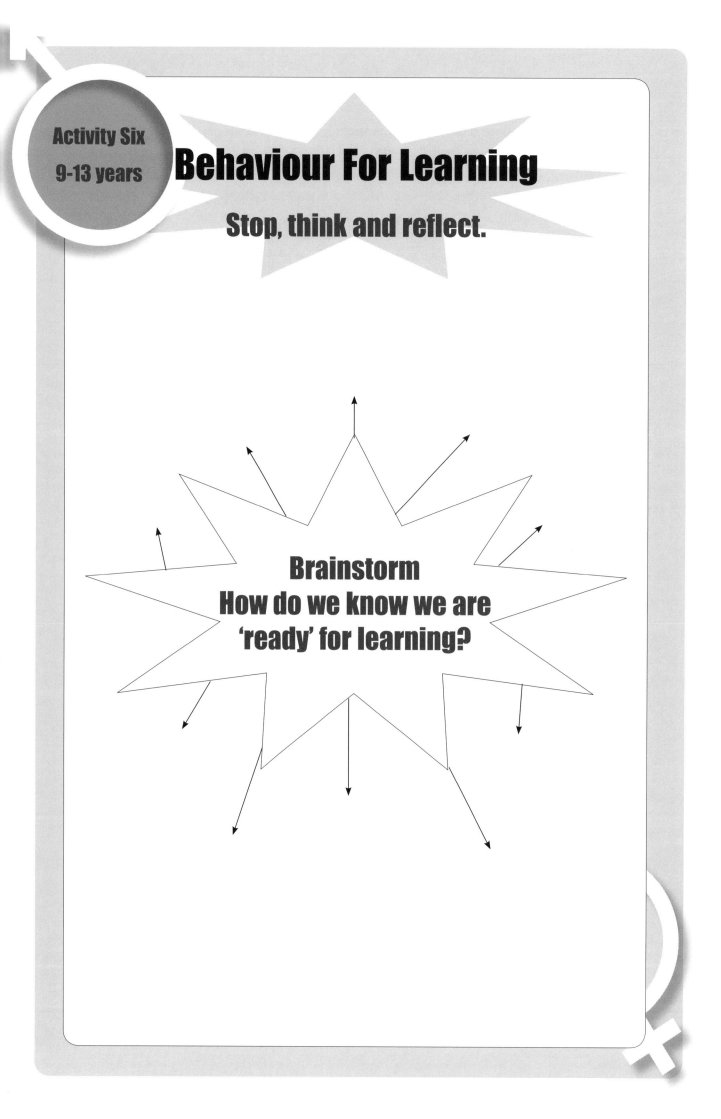

Behaviour For Learning

Stop, think and reflect.

**Brainstorm
How do we know we are
'ready' for learning?**

A Teacher's Quiz

Ask your teachers to reflect upon the following questions

1. Are boys and girls listed alphabetically in the school registers?

2. What criteria do you use for lining up?

3. Are you aware of the forms of address you use, for example, Head teacher, dinner lady, lollipop lady; different roles and responsibilities addressed differently for example. nursery teacher (Mrs Smith) /nursery nurse (Jane)?

4. Do you make sure parents are welcome and that communications are accessible?

5. Do you encourage pupils to work in mixed gender groups for classroom activities?

6. Do you think single sex groupings are sometimes more appropriate and, if so, when and why?

7. Do you have strategies to deal with cycles of dominant behaviour?

8. Do ALL pupils have the opportunity to participate fully e.g. in discussion, practical sessions.

9. Do you ensure equal access to all activities for boys and girls e.g. computer, cooking, football, etc

10. Do you encourage boys to do their fair share of tidying up and girls to lift and carry?

11. Do you ensure that pupils do not sit in single sex groups in assembly?

12. How do you ensure that your reactions to poor behaviour are not influenced by preconceived expectations regarding gender, ethnicity and ability?

Thank you for your thinking time!

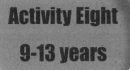

Assessment Stress!

Many people do not like tests, exam or assessments of any kind. Other people enjoy the experience of showing what they can do. What can you, your friends and your teachers do to make assessments less stressful? Ask them and record your ideas in the chart below:

Self	Friends	Teachers

Plan Your Ideal Lesson

Make a copy of this sheet and give it to your teacher. Then you can both plan your 'ideal' lesson. Remember to think about how everyone is included, different learning styles, e.g. visual, auditory, kinaesthetic, groupings (boys and girls) and how the classroom is set out. Good luck!

Lesson ....

Time	Activities	Resources	Groupings

How True Is This?

- Read and explain the following statement to a range of people.
- Include parents, carers, pupils and staff.
- Do they agree?
- Keep a record of how many do and do not agree.

'A curriculum informed by the principles of equal opportunities is essentially an inclusive curriculum, one which is accessible to all pupils, regardless of gender, class, ethnicity, ability or disability.'

(from Equal Opportunities in the Curriculum – London Borough of Hillingdon Education Services, October 1997 P.2.)

- Then ask how they think the curriculum can be made more inclusive in your school.
- Collect your information together, summarise and present!

Good luck!

Chapter Four

Communication, Language and Literacies

Introduction

In this chapter the focus is upon how we communicate with each other as social beings and the variety of methods by which we create meanings and get our messages across. The distinction between non-verbal and verbal communication is highlighted as is the need to be able to write and communicate to and for different audiences. In addition, the chapter explores the emotional importance of visual images and the way in which these are used in the media to put across specific points of view and encourage us to conform to certain views. Within this chapter there is also an emphasis on the diversity of ways in which people prefer to communicate, reinforcing the notion of difference and the idea that we need to develop respect for such difference in order to behave in a fair and inclusive manner towards each other. We also need to make sure that the ways in which we communicate are differentiated so as to include everyone regardless of gender, ethnicity, disability or ability, etc. With widespread recognition of gender differentiated responses to schooled literacies – the strategies recommended in this chapter provide a gender-fair approach to building classrooms where effective communication between all participants is the norm.

During recent years, the emphasis upon developing the skills of emotional literacy has been central to many PSHE and social curricular in schools. It is very important that all pupils and adults within a school community have access to and the opportunity to develop these kinds of skills, which allow them to communicate effectively and to manage their behaviours in a way that allows them to function appropriately in both the social and learning contexts. There is consequently a focus upon feelings and how we identify and manage these feelings and the ways in which we communicate them to each other. This includes attention to the ways in which we cope with anger and how we use anger in a productive way, i.e. being assertive as opposed to being aggressive when we encounter difficult situations. Overall, having the opportunity to develop these kinds of skills will advantage pupils and adults, both in and out of the school context.

Many people now recognise that emotional literacy, or emotional intelligence, is actually a better predictor for life-long achievement then is conventional IQ (Goleman: 1996). To develop this kind of literacy the kinds of competencies that need to develop include:

- self-awareness

- management of relationships

- motivation

- empathy or interpersonal sensitivity

- social skills

- emotional interactivity, that is putting all the above together

- conscientiousness and integrity (the individual's ability to accept personal responsibility and accountability for his/her actions and decisions alongside being open and transparent in their dealings with others).

For Peter Sharp (2001), the key to achieving these competencies initially lies in the individual's ability to develop a vision of themselves and who they want to be, that is the ideal self, and to then establish and work towards the necessary personal goals in order to achieve that end result – but within an orientation that builds empathy with others and good interpersonal skills.

How to use the activities

Note - For all ages, and especially for the younger age group, reading support might be needed. Where written responses are suggested, consider verbal feedback and circle time processes as alternatives.

Activity 1 – How Do We Communicate?

In this activity the pupils and facilitator can focus upon this question identifying the various ways in which we communicate with each other. Hopefully, a range of means will be identified, including the use of speaking and listening, reading and writing, use of electronic media, visual and verbal means and non-verbal means of communication, etc. The aim here is to reinforce the fact that we do not just communicate by talking and that we need to develop skills of observation and social interaction in order to really communicate most effectively. We need to be able to read others' body language and empathise with them if we are to truly initiate, develop and maintain positive relationships with others.

The 5-8 year old group are presented with a differentiated version of this activity called Get In Touch!. Pupils are asked to draw and label the different ways in which they communicate with each other. Three examples are provided as a prompt. The teacher may wish to complete the activity via a whole class discussion with the younger pupils, enlarging the worksheet to A3 size and acting as a scribe for the pupil's ideas.

Activity 2 – Communication Activities

The teacher presents three activities that encourage pupils to communicate in three different ways: verbally, non-verbally and visually. The activities are clearly explained on the sheet and may require reinforcement subsequent to this initial introduction. They are fun ways of introducing some quite complex ideas and hopefully pupils should enjoy engaging in these activities.

The activities for the 5-8 year old group have the same objectives in terms of showing how we communicate in different ways and providing opportunities to practice these skills. However, the first two activities are perhaps more appropriate to the younger age range.

Activity 3 – Writing for difference audiences

In this activity pupils are asked to consider how they would write a text message to say they were ill and wouldn't be attending school that day to four different people – your best friend, your teacher, your parent/carer and the school administrator. This activity aims to reinforce the ways in which we may write and communicate differently to different audiences and the need to be able to develop skills that allow us to do this confidently.

The younger pupils are asked to write or draw a postcard to four different people as follows: a best friend, a teacher, a parent or carer or an older relative or friend. The teacher can act as a scribe for the younger pupils and record their ideas on to the postcards once they have completed the pictures.

Activity 4 - Visual Communication

In this activity the facilitator is asked to select six images from recent newspaper articles/events in the media. Those presented on the activity sheet are merely intended as examples but could be used if it is not possible to collect the information within the given time frame. The images should be powerful, e.g. a child starving in its mother's arms or the twin towers being blown apart. The Circle Time forum can then be used to focus on what feelings these images engender and to question why they should be so powerful. The main purpose of the activity is to reinforce the powerful nature of visual imagery and the ways in which our emotional responses to an image can sometimes possibly prevent us from analysing it accurately and understanding the issues better, for example, identifying the causes.

The 5-8 year old group are also presented with six visual images from newspapers or magazines. They are also asked to consider how these make them feel and why they should or might engender such strong feelings. Pupils are asked to question if they would experience the same strength of feeling if they had simply heard about these events and not actually seen them. The discussion is conducted via a Circle Time approach. It may be helpful to reduce the number if images presented to the younger pupils and perhaps allocate separate discussion times for each one.

Activity 5 - Say What You Mean

In this activity the pupils are presented with a scenario concerning a boy with Asperger's syndrome who tends to take things that are said to him very literally. This causes him and others around him some difficulties and problems. The pupils are asked to work together in groups in order to identify the kinds of things that we say that might confuse him and what can be done to be supportive. They are asked to consider not only other pupils who may be on the autistic continuum but to also consider those who have only recently started to speak in English – where making sense of the meanings others are communicating may be challenging. Central to this activity is reinforcement of the importance of including others and in differentiating the way in which we communicate in order to do so most effectively.

The 5-8 year old group are presented with a scenario in which a boy arrives at their school with very little English language. They are asked to consider how they might help him and how they would communicate with him. The teacher can present this activity as part of a circle discussion and act as a scribe for the younger pupil's ideas and suggestions.

Activity 6 - Communicate Your Feelings

In this activity the pupils are asked to identify as many different feelings as they can within a short time-frame, i.e. how many different feelings do we have? They are then asked to consider which of these they find comfortable and uncomfortable and to identify and clarify ways in which they deal most effectively with uncomfortable feelings. The idea here is to reinforce the importance of being able to talk about feelings and also being able to manage them most effectively so that they don't prevent us from being motivated and engaging in learning and social contexts.

The activity for the younger age group requires the pupils to brainstorm the range of feelings that they experience on a daily basis. They are then required to colour code these feelings, distinguishing between uncomfortable and comfortable feelings. They are finally asked to identify how they might help both themselves and others with the uncomfortable feelings. The teacher may need to act as a scribe for the younger pupils. It may also be useful to have a red and a yellow box so that pupils can 'post' their feelings into each one.

Activity 7 - Investigate The Anger

The activity leads directly on from Activity 6 in that most of the pupils and the facilitator/teacher will probably have identified anger as a feeling that is often quite uncomfortable and more difficult to deal with than other feelings. Pupils are required to ask a range of individuals what actually triggers their anger and how it affects them and others around them and what they'd like to be able to do in order to deal with anger more effectively. Pupils are asked to question themselves, their teacher, a friend and parent/carer. The idea here is to reinforce the fact that all human beings, boys and girls, encounter this emotion and most human beings will have some difficulties at some point in their lives in dealing effectively with such uncomfortable feelings and situations. However, this commonality also occurs within the ways in which we deal with such feelings and it is intended here that everyone is given the opportunity to share strategies and empathise with one another.

The activity for the 5-8 year old group asks the pupils to draw out their anger. They are required to identify the situation, what they did, what others did and how everyone felt. They are also asked to say what they would like to do next time if they encountered a similar difficulty. Reception aged pupils can simply draw a picture of themselves feeling angry and then talk through the situation with their teacher.

Activity 8 - Effective Communication

In this activity pupils are asked to discuss and prepare definitions for being assertive, being aggressive and being passive. The aim here is to reinforce the fact that the most effective communication occurs when we are comfortably assertive with one another as opposed to being aggressive or passive. This activity allows pupils and their teacher/facilitator to change some behavioural patterns that may tend to be gender specific and oppressive.

The younger pupils are asked to draw and label themselves asking for their ball back in an aggressive, an assertive and a passive manner. Opportunities to act out each response may help to prompt the younger pupils. Each behaviour can initially be modelled by the teacher.

Activity 9 - Practise your skills

This activity leads directly on from Activity 8 in that the pupils are asked to work in pairs or small groups in order to work out assertive responses to a range of problem situations. Many of the situations involve the teacher feeling threatened or undermined and this is considered particularly important so that the pupils can understand the feelings and perspective of someone in a position of authority. Once again, there is an emphasis on the mutuality of our emotions and feelings and the way in which we all encounter difficult and complex emotions on a daily basis. It is how we manage these difficult emotions and problem situations that is important and the kind of strategies and techniques that we use will probably be common across the genders and throughout the age ranges, i.e. very similar for a teacher as for a pupil. If we feel threatened, undermined, hurt or abused, then we will all react in similar ways and consequently we all need to develop a range of similar strategies and techniques in order to deal with such complex emotions and situations.

The younger pupils, on the sheet 'Saying What You want', are presented with a range of problems more suited to the younger age group and are asked to work out assertive responses to the situations. They are then required to act out the scenarios with a partner. Reception pupils can be presented with these via a whole class circle discussion and the teacher can model responses and act as a partner to individual pupils as appropriate.

Activity 10 - Our School

This final activity is really an opportunity for pupils and staff/facilitators to be self-reflective. They are asked to look at the front entrance of the school and to consider what it actually communicates to people who come in from the outside. Is it warm, friendly, safe, exciting and welcoming and does it tell you what actually goes on in the school and who is involved? Does it also let you see that children and adults of different genders, ethnicities, abilities, etc., can work and learn together in a truly collegiate and inclusive manner? The pupils are asked to do their own research and to come back and feed back as part of the whole group. This is very important as they are being asked to participate fully and to have their voices heard. What is also important, however, as a follow on from this, is that should any discrepancies or problems be encountered on uncovered, these must be addressed via the Senior Management Team and staff within the school in partnership with the pupils.

The final part of the activity asks the pupils to present how they would like their schools' front entrance to look and what they want it to communicate. It may be helpful to make a display of these designs and to reinforce to all involved in the curriculum how important it is to incorporate the pupils' views and understand that their perceptions really do have value and credibility. They need to feel that they can, and do, contribute to what their school is communicating to the outside world.

This activity is differentiated for the 5-8 year old group who are also asked to design the front entrance to their school. They are asked to ensure that it is warm, friendly, exciting, welcoming to all and shows how they all work and play together. Reception aged pupils can complete the drawing and then discuss their ideas and designs with the teacher.

Practical strategies

Ten A4 activity sheets for 5-8 year olds:

Activity 1   – Get In Touch

Activity 2   – Communication Activities

Activity 3   – A Postcard To….

Activity 4   – Visual Communication

Activity 5   – Say What You Mean

Activity 6   – My Feelings

Activity 7   – Draw Your Anger

Activity 8   – Saying What You Want

Activity 9   – Using Your Skills

Activity 10 – Our School.

Ten A4 activity sheets for 9-13 year olds:

Activity 1   – How Do We Communicate?

Activity 2   – Communication Activities

Activity 3   – Writing For Difference Audiences

Activity 4   – Visual Communication

Activity 5   – Say What You Mean

Activity 6   – Communicate Your Feelings

Activity 7   – Investigate The Anger

Activity 8   – Effective Communication

Activity 9   – Practise Your Skills

Activity 10 – Our School

Further references and resources

Dwivedi, K. and Harper, P. (1999) *Promoting the Emotional Well-being of Children and Adolescents and Preventing Their Mental Ill Health: a Handbook.* London and Philadelphia: Jessica Kingsley Publishers.

Faupel, A. Herrick, E. and Sharp, P. (1998) *Anger Management – A Practical Guide.* London: David Fulton Publishers.

Goleman, D. (1996) *Emotional Intelligence: Why it can matter more than IQ.* London: Bloomsbury.

McConnon, S. (1990) *Conflict – A Personal Skills Course for Young People.* London: MacMillan.

Rae, T. (2004) *Emotional Survival – An Emotional Literacy Course for High School Students.* Bristol: Lucky Duck Publishing.

Sharp, P. (2001) *Nurturing Emotional Literacy: a practical guide for teachers, parents and those in the caring professions.* London: David Fulton Publishing.

Stacey, H. and Robinson, P. (1997) *Let's Mediate – A Teacher's Guide to Peer Support and Conflict Resolution Skills for all Ages.* Bristol: Lucky Duck Publishing.

Tamarind Ltd, AMS Educational Woodside Trading Estate, Low Lane, Horsforth, Leeds LS18 5NY - Wide range of multicultural books and story books which address disability in a straightforward and sensitive ma*nner.*

The Emotional Literacy Handbook Promoting Whole-school Strategies. London: David Fulton Publishers in association with Antidote Campaign for Emotional Literacy.

Reflection and next steps

- It may be helpful for school staff to consider developing a policy on the ways in which they communicate effectively or otherwise to parents/carers. It could be useful to conduct a survey in order ascertain whether or not parents/carers do find the school accessible and feel that information provided to them is presented in a clear, concise, user friendly and non-stereotypical fashion.

- Pupils could conduct a survey to ascertain how many different languages are spoken in home contexts. Have the school provided these parents/carers with information in their own language? If not, this is something that could be worked on so as to ensure that all school documentation, including letters, information sheets, etc, can be translated. What is the possibility of providing school booklets/information booklets in home languages? Is this something that pupils themselves could work on with the help of older siblings? Would the school consider setting up such a volunteer system whereby parents/carers who were literate could support the school in developing information leaflets in home languages, etc.

- It may be helpful to consider incorporating an anger management programme into the PSHE/ Emotional Literacy programme. Although pupils may have access to the DfES SEALS (Social and Emotional Aspects of Learning) curriculum, it may well be the case that further work and reinforcement of positive means of coping effectively with stronger, uncomfortable feelings will be necessary. A resource such as *Crucial Skills An Anger Management and Problem Solving Teaching Programme* by Penny Johnson and Tina Rae (1999) may be helpful in supporting staff in planning and developing such a resource. Although this programme is aimed at pupils who are experiencing difficulty in managing anger in areas of conflict, it will probably be the case that the majority of pupils will experience such difficulties at some point in their school careers and would therefore benefit from such an approach.

- It may be helpful to consider whether mentoring, either by teachers or older pupils or the school mentor may be appropriate for some pupils who do present with particular difficulties in this area.

Get In Touch!

How do we do this?

Draw and label. The first three are done for you!

We get in touch by:

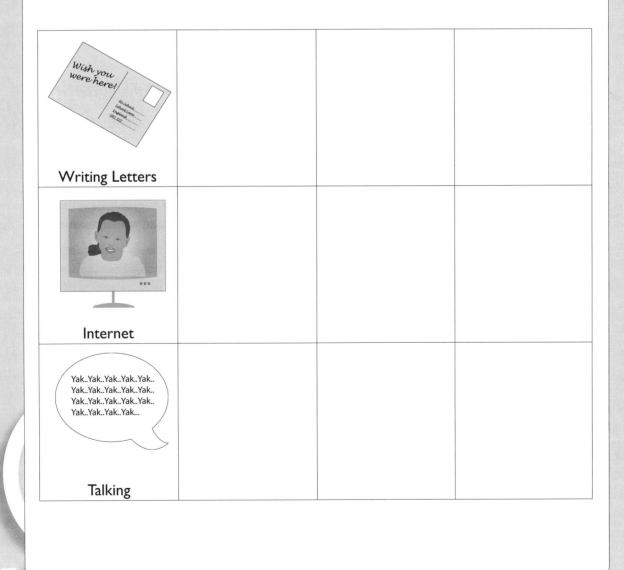

Writing Letters			
Internet			
Talking			

Communication Activities

The Winking Game

The facilitator nominates one person to be the Winker. The other pupils are not aware of the choice. Children sit as for circle time and the Winker begins to wink. Once winked at, the children have to 'pretend' to fall asleep. The Winker has to stop if he or she is caught out by another participant.

The Whispering Game

The children sit as for Circle Time. A message is passed around the circle by a child who is nominated by the facilitator when the message reaches the end of the circle, the child who receives it is required to state it aloud. This message is then compared to the original message. Another child can then be nominated to have a go!

Draw My Picture!

One pupil is asked to volunteer and stand with his or her back to the class and to describe a picture that he or she has drawn. This can be simple and composed of geometric shapes (especially for the first attempt!) The pupil can only use words to describe the image whilst the rest of the class attempt to reproduce the image on individual sheets of paper. The activity can be repeated (time allowing) with other volunteers.

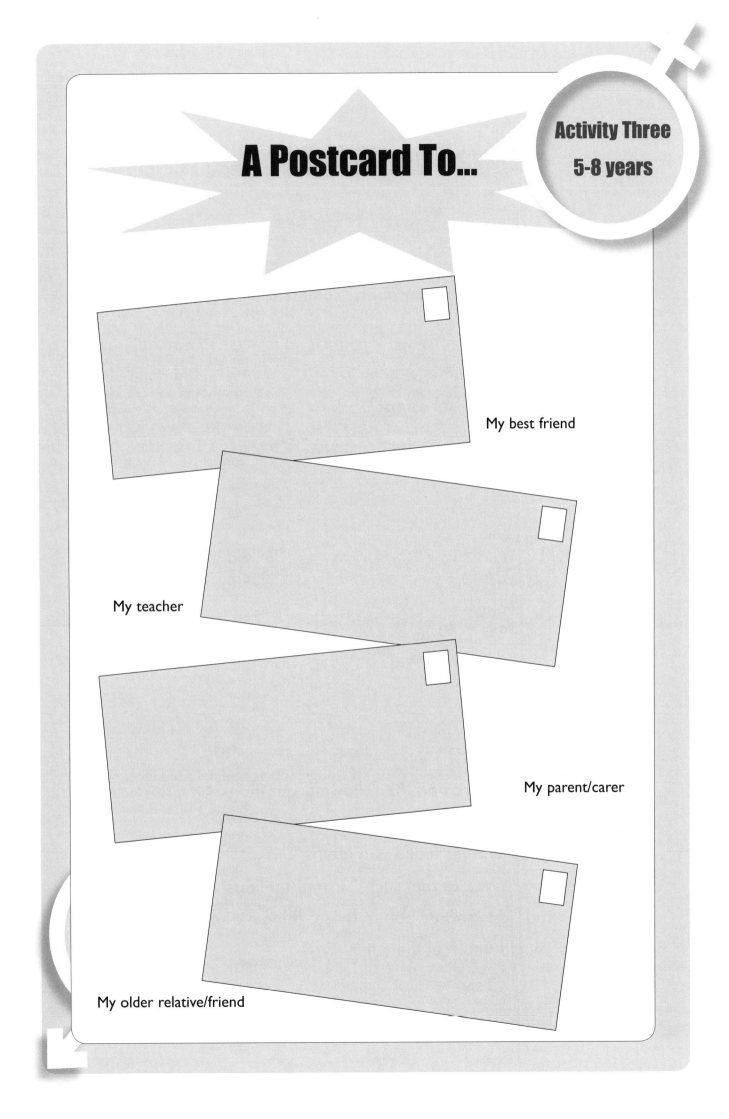

A Postcard To...

My best friend

My teacher

My parent/carer

My older relative/friend

Visual Communication

Select six images from newspapers, some examples are:

A child who is lost in a large town

A child being bullied by a gang

A starving woman

An old man being mugged

People trying to escape a house fire

Devastation left after a hurricane

Use Circle Time to focus on the following questions:

- How do these images make you feel?
- Why do they make us feel such 'strong' feelings?
- If you had just heard about these things and not seen the pictures, would you feel the same way?

Say What You Mean!

Hamid is a new boy. He has just arrived in the UK and he cannot speak English.

How would you help him?

How would you communicate with him?

Write and draw your ideas.

My Feelings

Colour code: red   = uncomfortable

                   yellow = comfortable

Circle questions

- How do you cope with your uncomfortable feelings?

- Who can help us?

- How can we help ourselves?

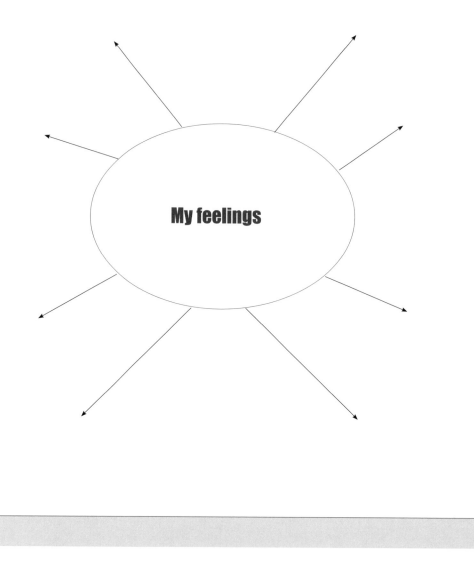

My feelings

Investigate The Anger

I was angry when...	I did...
Other people did...	I felt...
They felt...	What I'd like to do next time

!**!?@!!**

Saying What You Want!

Draw and label yourself asking another child to give you your ball back in three ways:

1. Assertively
2. Aggressively
3. Passively.

1. Assertively	2. Aggressively	3. Passively

Practise Your Skills

Work out an assertive response to the following problems:

One child fouling another in a football match.

Older girl snatching younger girls mobile phone.

Boy being tripped up in dinner queue.

Two boys refusing to let girl join in their game.

Teacher telling off child for talking when it wasn't him or her.

Child being bullied because he is small and Asian.

Child unable to do his or her work and getting upset.

Child in playground left out at side of game but wanting to join.

Child being cuddled by an adult and not liking it.

Act it out with a partner!

Our School

Design the front entrance to your school. Make it warm, friendly, exciting and welcoming to all. Make sure it shows how you work and play together.

My Design

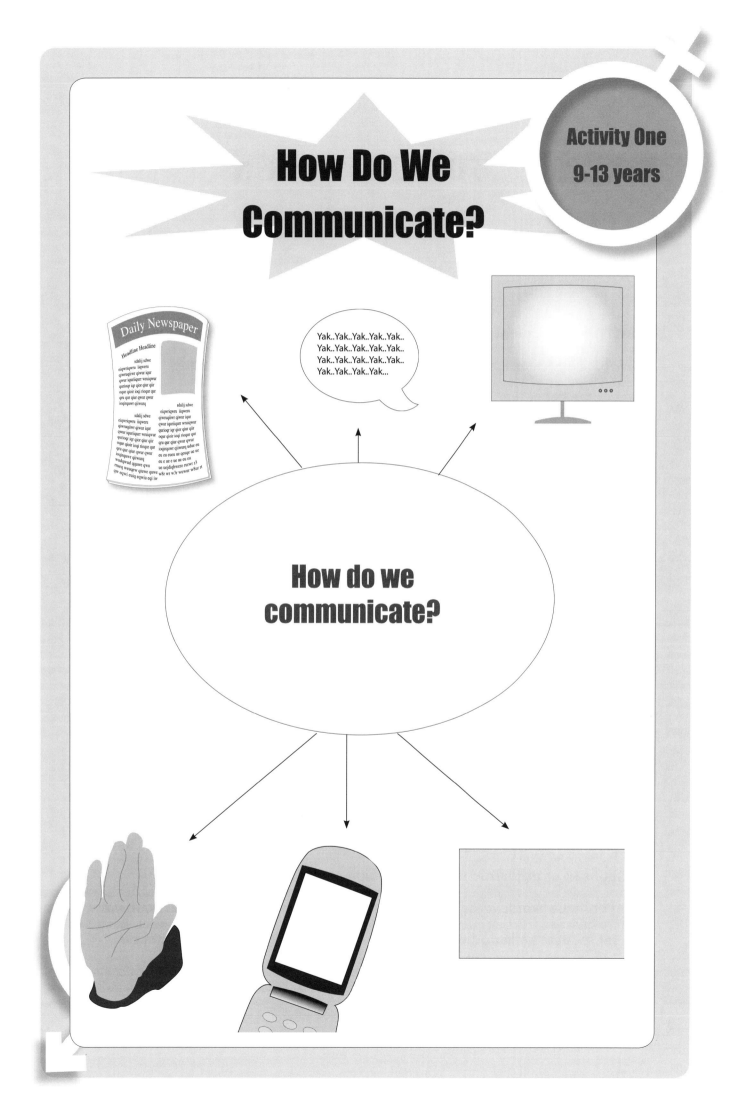

Communication Activities

Activity (1) Guess Who?

The facilitator nominates one person to leave the room. Whilst this pupil is out of the room, the facilitator nominates another student to be 'it'. The first pupil returns to the room and is encouraged to ask questions of his or her classmates in order to find out who is 'it'. The students are only allowed to answer 'yes', 'no' or 'I don't know' and this continues until the pupil has been able to guess and identify correctly.

Activity (2) Sign Up!

Pupils are each allocated a partner. The task is for each pupil to try to explain to their partner how they are feeling through the use of mime. Once they have 'mimed their feelings' the partner is asked to guess the feeling. Both pupils can have a go at miming and guessing.

Activity (3) Draw it Out!

One pupil is asked to volunteer and stand with his or her back to the class and to describe a picture that he or she has drawn. This can be simple and composed of geometric shapes (especially for the first attempt!) The pupil can only use words to describe the image whilst the rest of the class attempt to reproduce the image on individual sheets of paper. The activity can be repeated (time allowing) with other volunteers.

Writing For Different Audiences

How would you text a message to say you were ill and wouldn't be attending school that day to:

(a) Your best friend	(b) Your teacher
(c) Your parent or carer	(d) The school administrator

Visual Communication

Select six images from newspapers, some examples are:

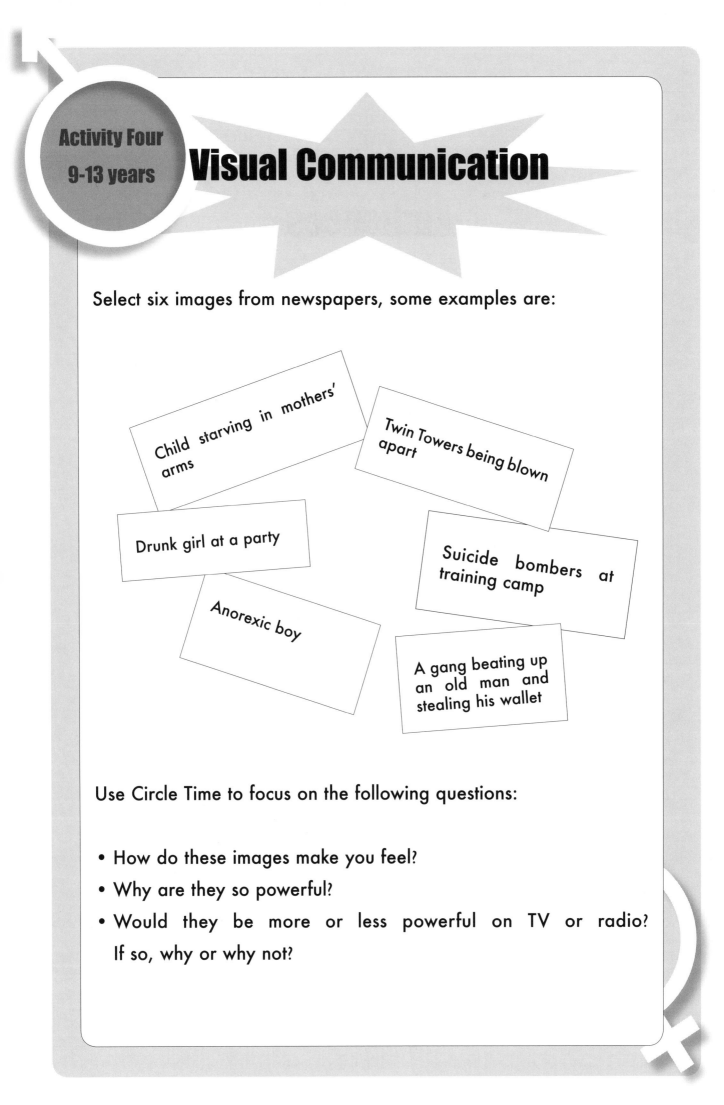

Child starving in mothers' arms

Twin Towers being blown apart

Drunk girl at a party

Suicide bombers at training camp

Anorexic boy

A gang beating up an old man and stealing his wallet

Use Circle Time to focus on the following questions:

- How do these images make you feel?
- Why are they so powerful?
- Would they be more or less powerful on TV or radio? If so, why or why not?

Say What You Mean!

Group Activity

Scenario

Albert has Asperger's syndrome. He tends to take things you say literally. For example, if someone says 'I'll crack your nuts' he looks around, confused because he hasn't got any nuts and can't see any in the immediate vicinity. This often leads to problems.

Task

Work together and try to identify the things we say that might confuse someone like Albert or alternatively someone who has only recently started to speak English. Record your ideas on this sheet and then feedback to the whole group.

Our ideas

Brainstorm ways of trying to minimise the confusion and maximising the support for him

Communicate Your Feelings

How many different feelings do we have?

Record as many as you can in five minutes!

Stop, think and reflect.

- Which feelings do you find comfortable?
- Which feelings do you find uncomfortable?
- How do you currently cope with your uncomfortable feelings?
- Do you think you could cope better?
- Who could help you in this and how do you think you could help yourself?

Investigate the Anger

Assess yourself and others. What makes you feel angry? What are your triggers? How can you cope more effectively? Self reflect and ask others.

Self

Triggers
What I do
How it affects me
How it affects others
What I'd LIKE to do

Teacher

Triggers
What I do
How it affects me
How it affects others
What I'd LIKE to do

Friend

Triggers
What I do
How it affects me
How it affects others
What I'd LIKE to do

Parent or carer

Triggers
What I do
How it affects me
How it affects others
What I'd LIKE to do

- Discuss in your group! Look at the similarities and differences.
- What can we ALL do to help ourselves and each other communicate our anger more effectively?

Effective Communication

Discuss and prepare definitions for the following ways of communicating:

(1) Being assertive

(2) Being aggressive

(3) Being passive

Discuss and agree in your group.

Being assertive is
You look
You sound
You feel
You get

Being aggressive is
You look
You sound
You feel
You get

Being passive is
You look
You sound
You feel
You get

Practise Your Skills

Work in pairs or small groups and work out an ASSERTIVE response to these problem situations. You may have to switch roles, for example, from pupil to teacher and vice versa.

Your teacher likes boys better than girls and never gives you a chance to do practicals in his lessons.

Two students in your class are really aggressive and try to shout over you every time you start a new lesson or topic.

You have been asked to tidy up the Art room but the boys are never asked.

People keep saying you look fat and you feel fed up with it.

You are fed up in the Maths lesson because nothing is ever explained properly.

You got a detention for mucking about in class but it wasn't really you.

Two girls in your group keep trying to take your mobile phone.

Your Mum thinks you are lazy but you just don't find the work easy.

The Head teacher saw you get upset when your class was badly behaved and now thinks you're a useless teacher.

You have spent hours preparing a good lesson for your class and 2 students are determined to ruin it – you don't know why.

You lost your homework but the teach doesn't believe you at all.

Your best friend wants you to smoke and drink when you go out but you're not interested.

Our School
What Do We Say?

Look at your front entrance to the school. What does it communicate? Is it warm, friendly, safe, exciting and welcoming? Does it tell you about what goes on and who is involved? Does it let you see how boys and girls of different cultures and races work and learn together? Check it out – ASK QUESTIONS!

What would you like your school's front entrance to communicate? Stop, think, reflect and then draw and label.

Chapter Five

Families, Communities and the Wider World

Introduction

The main focus of this chapter is upon emphasising, highlighting and valuing difference, promoting a truly inclusive school culture and at the same time exploring ways to widen opportunities now and in the future.. There is particular focus on people who participate in work in the community and the roles that they play. Pupils are asked to consider the usefulness of certain jobs and the way in which they may, or may not be, gender specific. It is really important that they are given the opportunity to question the ways in which certain jobs are designated to each gender alongside beginning to think about why girls and boys are treated differently and chanelled into different ways of behaving and being by their peers and the adults who care for them – and what some of the consequences may be of this gender polarisation.

This is particularly important, given the fact that there is generally a feeling that many boys, in particular, are emotionally mis-educated. This mis-education takes place within the family, the peer group and within the entertainment industry and we need to be very careful that schools are not in some respects 'anti-boy'. Schools historically have generally tended to emphasise reading and writing and restricted the activity of younger boys who, for a variety of reasons, tend to be more active and slower to read than girls. Teachers have often disciplined boys more harshly than girls and it seems that sensitivity has not been modelled to boys so they consequently have not learnt how to manifest sensitivity themselves.

It is very important that the pupils begin to question such distinctions and consider how they are responded to and whether or not this is in fact entirely appropriate. It is also, of course, equally important that boys are encouraged to not hide behind a mask of bravado and to be able to develop the kinds of emotional vocabularies and strategies that allow them to deal with jeering, insults and confrontation in both the school and social context. It is vital, even at this early stage, that both pupils and those caring for them become increasingly more aware of the need to develop the mental and emotional wellbeing of boys in particular. This is vital given the fact that boys are much more likely than girls to hurt or kill themselves or each other. Without the skills of emotional literacy or intelligence, boys miss the opportunity to gain mastery over their inner lives. The activities within this chapter should, hopefully, begin to raise awareness whilst also allowing and enabling the pupils to begin to develop the skills that they may need and not have developed appropriately to date. There includes an exploration of the role of parents and the importance of developing sound parenting and nurturing skills.

The final focus in this chapter is upon identifying future paths and worlds and it is particularly important that the pupils are encouraged to consider the kind of man or woman that they would want to be in the future and not to have their dreams and aspirations limited by socially unjust learning cultures which do not counter the five faces of oppression:

victimisation, marginalisation, violence, powerlessness and exploitation (Young: 1990).

How to use the activity sheets

Note - For all ages, and especially for the younger age group, reading support might be needed. Where written responses are suggested, consider verbal feedback and circle time processes as alternatives.

Activity 1 - What Do We Know About Our Cultures?

In this activity pupils and facilitator(s) are asked to identify as many facts as they can about the different cultures they belong to. They are then asked to consider any similarities and differences. The idea here is to reinforce the notion of difference and the importance of respecting and tolerating these differences. It is vital that this is not a superficial respect, that is merely on the surface and masking underlying prejudices and hatreds. If we are to be in a truly inclusive school community and society, then we need to truly embrace one another. In this way we can also empower each other and ensure that everyone's voice is heard and no one is abused or excluded.

The activity for the 5-8 year old group is entitled 'Different People' and pupils are asked to draw and label how they are different and how they are the same. It may be appropriate for the teacher to record the younger pupil's responses. These can be elicited via a whole class circle discussion and recorded on an enlarged version of the worksheet.

Activity 2 - Investigation

This activity asks the pupils to find out about a culture that is different to their own. They are asked to interview a friend or a member of staff and make up a questionnaire which includes a range of different issues such as how significant events are celebrated, the role of women, the role of men, attitudes towards education, etc. The aim here is to reinforce the importance of respecting difference but also eliciting truly accurate information. Merely resorting to reference books and other published materials is not always useful – we need to gather information about other cultures from people who belong to those cultures and can give a living picture of what it means to be a part of that group.

The younger pupils are required to find out about someone who is different to themselves. This is presented as a quiz and a range of headings are provided to prompt thinking and the formulation of appropriate questions. The pupils are then asked to design a poster in order to illustrate what they have found out. Reception aged pupils can draw a picture of someone who is different to them and then discuss these differences with the teacher.

Activity 3 - People Who Help

In this Circle Time session a selection of pictures are presented to the pupils and they are asked to identify the people and what they do and to also clarify how they actually help others in the role that they have chosen to adopt. These include: a doctor, a chef, a mechanic, etc. It is very important that any images presented do not reinforce stereotypes. Pupils are presented with images that reinforce the fact that a range of jobs should be and can be available to both genders and that choices needn't and shouldn't be limited by your sexual orientation.

The activity is the same for the younger age group although the questions have been simplified and the sheet is called 'Guess Who?'.

Activity 4 - Positive and Negative Parenting and Caring

In this activity the pupils are asked to consider what makes a positive parent or carer and to identify the qualities and attributes of a positive parent or carer. Pupil's contributions will be many and varied and may include some of the following: parents/carers will need to provide financially, provide love, give boundaries, act as a role model, teach social skills, provide physical and material goods, look after you and stick up for you, etc. Negative qualities may include not nurturing your self-esteem, putting you down, not looking after you physically, not providing for you physically or emotionally, not reading to you or looking after you when you are little. This activity may raise some difficult emotions for those children who have poor care at home – and this will need to be handled sensitively. A follow-up activity is to explore how they themselves might develop these positive skills and attitudes when they become a parent themselves.

The 5-8 year old group are asked to draw and label pictures of positive parents and carers. They are asked to identify the qualities of someone who would be good at looking after them and someone who would not be good at taking on this role. Reception aged pupils can discuss their ideas with the teacher once they have completed each picture.

Activity 5 – Boys and Girls – What Are They Made Of?

In this activity the pupils are asked to consider the ways in which people in the past may have tried to make little boys and girls different to each other by rewarding them or allowing them to gain attention for doing different things. There is a sense in which boys have been expected to be noisy, aggressive, tough, brave and not cry, whilst girls have been expected to be soft and gentle, interested in looking after babies, enjoying tidying up, being pretty and playing quietly. This is a particularly important activity in that the pupils are being asked to consider and reflect upon the way in which adults treated them when they were small and whether or not this may have impacted on the way they are now as human beings, particularly in the ways in which they behave, learn and respond to others within relationships. There is an emphasis on the fact that children who may have been raised to be noisy and aggressive may also then find it particularly difficult to cope in a classroom where a teacher values and prizes those who play quietly and show no aggressive or noisy tendencies. There is an obvious gender dimension to this dynamic.

The younger pupils are asked to draw a girl playing and a boy playing and then to focus on a series of questions via a Circle Time discussion. They are required to identify differences and to also consider and discuss if the two groups have to be different.

Activity 6 – Investigate Your Games

In this activity the pupils are asked to consider a range of different games, toys and activities that they may have used in the past or may currently be using. They are asked to focus on whether or not these games are likely to make them noisy, prompt them to fight, make them want to feel better than others, make them want to look after others, make them feel self-conscious and worry about being attractive, make them want to run around, make them want to be quiet, make them want to feel happy or make them want to feel friendly. The aim here is to reinforce the fact that some games do produce and encourage more anti-social behaviours and perhaps we need to be more reflective about the games and activities we encourage children to participate in, particularly if we want to promote the notion of emotionally literate, empathic and socially well-adjusted young people.

The 5-8 year old group are presented with a series of images representing a variety of games. They are required to colour code the activities, sorting them out into those that might encourage them to become noisy, fight, be quiet, kind and friendly. It may be helpful to make this activity more practical for Reception aged pupils by setting a series of large plastic hoops, for example, red representing noisy games, yellow representing quiet games etc. The pupils can then cut out the pictures and place each one in the appropriate hoop or category. They can then discuss their thinking with the teacher.

Activity 7 - Problem Card - A Boys' Problem

This activity is directly related to the previous two activities in that it focuses on a little boy who was having difficulty in maintaining appropriate behaviours in the school context. The pupils are asked to read the scenario prior to answering a series of questions. There is a focus here on boys becoming emotionally literate and developing the ability to talk about their feelings. The emphasis is upon the importance of providing boys with frameworks and opportunities to do this as opposed to bottling up emotions, particularly given that research has shown that this does lead in later life to problems with mental health and wellbeing.

captions for a story board are presented to the younger age group in which a boy becomes aggressive in a football game. The pupils are asked to consider a series of questions and to particularly identify what might help this boy in the future. Reception aged pupils can discuss these questions with the teacher who can talk them through the cartoon story first.

Activity 8 - Survey The Group

This is an investigative activity in which all the pupils are asked to identify future careers and to state the reason why they would choose such a career. The pupils are asked to consider whether or not the boys and girls in the group have actually chosen similar careers or jobs and to consider why this might be so.

The activity for the 5-8 year old group asks pupils to identify what they want to be when they grow up and then to compare their choices with friends of both genders. Reception aged pupils can simply complete the drawings and these can then be pinned to a display board so as to act as a prompt to the whole group discussion.

Activity 9 - What Influences Us In Our Worlds?

The pupils are presented with a series of statements that they are asked to place in order of importance, i.e. which person influences me most and which person influences me least. They are then asked to compare their rankings with a friend and discuss any similarities and differences.

The younger group are presented with the same activity, called 'My World' but in picture form. They are asked to cut out the pictures and then sequence them in order of influence. This activity could be completed in a whole class group with the teacher leading the discussion and eliciting the pupil's views. This would make the activity more practical for the younger pupils. It may also be helpful to limit the number of picture cards to be discussed for the Reception aged pupils.

Activity 10 - The Sky's The Limit

This is a final Circle Time session in which pupils focus upon their future goals and dreams. There is an emphasis on identifying the kind of man or woman that they would like to be when they are grown up. It is hoped that the gender-aware nature of the activities to date will help to inform the pupils' choices and judgements. It is also hoped that the pupils will feel empowered to reach their goals whilst also respecting and tolerating the goals and views of others.

The activity is the same for both age groups but entitled 'My Future' for the younger group. The teacher may wish to focus upon the concepts of targets and goals prior to completing the activity. This may be particularly important for the younger pupils who may not have experienced this language previously.

Practical strategies

Ten A4 activity sheets for 5-8 year olds:

Activity 1   – Different People

Activity 2   – A Quiz

Activity 3   – Guess Who?

Activity 4   – Positive Parents and Carers

Activity 5   – Boys and Girls

Activity 6   – Our Games

Activity 7   – A Problem – Adam's Anger

Activity 8   – When I Grow Up

Activity 9   – My World

Activity 10 – My Future

Ten A4 activity sheets for 9-13 year olds:

Activity 1   – What Do We Know About Our Cultures?

Activity 2   – Investigation

Activity 3   – People Who Help

Activity 4   – Positive and Negative Parenting

Activity 5   – Boys and Girls

Activity 6   – Investigate Your Games

Activity 7   – When I Grow Up...

Activity 8   – Survey the group

Activity 9   – What Influences Us In Our Worlds?

Activity 10 – My Future

Further references and resources

Anderson, J. Beels, C. and Powell, D .(1994) *Health Skills for Life: Health Education and PSE Materials for Key Stage 3.* London: Thomas Nelson and Sons Ltd.

Kindlon, E. and Thompson, M. (1999) *Raising Cain – Protecting the Emotional Life of Boys.* London: Penguin Books.

Letterbox Library Unit, 2D Leroy House, 436 Essex Road, London N1 3QP – specialists in non-sexist and multicultural books.

Mantra Publishing, 5 Alexandra Grove, London N12 8NU – Multicultural resources and dual language books. Picture books available in twenty languages.

Rae, T. Nelson, L. and Pedersen, L. (2005) *Developing Emotional Literacy with Teenage Girls – building confidence, self-esteem and self-respect.* Bristol: Lucky Duck Publishing.

Salisbury, J. and Jackson, D. (1996) *Challenging Macho Values – practical ways of working with adolescent boys.* London: Falmer Press.

Reflection and next steps

- It may be useful to include parents/carers in work on parenting skills in order to really bring the topic alive and make it more meaningful for those involved. Parents and carers could contribute by giving talks to different year groups, discussing their role and the difficulties, challenges and rewards that it holds for them.

- Allocate some additional time for staff to consider particularly the ways in which boys do or do not dominate the physical and psychological space in the school context. This is particularly important given that this kind of domination often prevents girls from fully participating in, and making use of, school resources in developing their own lives and careers. What is the school's policy for ensuring ongoing anti-sexist work with boys? What is the policy on ensuring that the curriculum is not gender biased in either direction? It may also be helpful to look closely at the resources and representations in the school, i.e. what versions of masculinity and femininity are being promoted? It could be that staff can identify ways of diversifying this and further challenging existing stereotypes.

- It may also be helpful to consider developing group work with a particular focus on fostering the emotional literacy of both boys and girls in the school context. This may require consideration as to grouping, i.e. some boys or girls may be better targeted in single sex groups for this kind of work. There are copious resources now available in order to begin to foster such skills in young people, including *Emotional Survival: An emotional literacy course for High School Students* by Tina Rae (2004) and *Developing Emotional Literacy with Teenage Girls: Building Confidence Self-esteem and Self-respect* by Tina Rae, Lorna Nelson and Lisa Pedersen (2005).

- It may be useful to particularly focus on homophobic attitudes within the school context and to conduct further awareness raising sessions in order to dispel existing myths and prejudices. This should include listening to the voices of gay and lesbian pupils and staff.

Different People

Draw and label:

How are we different?	How are we the same?

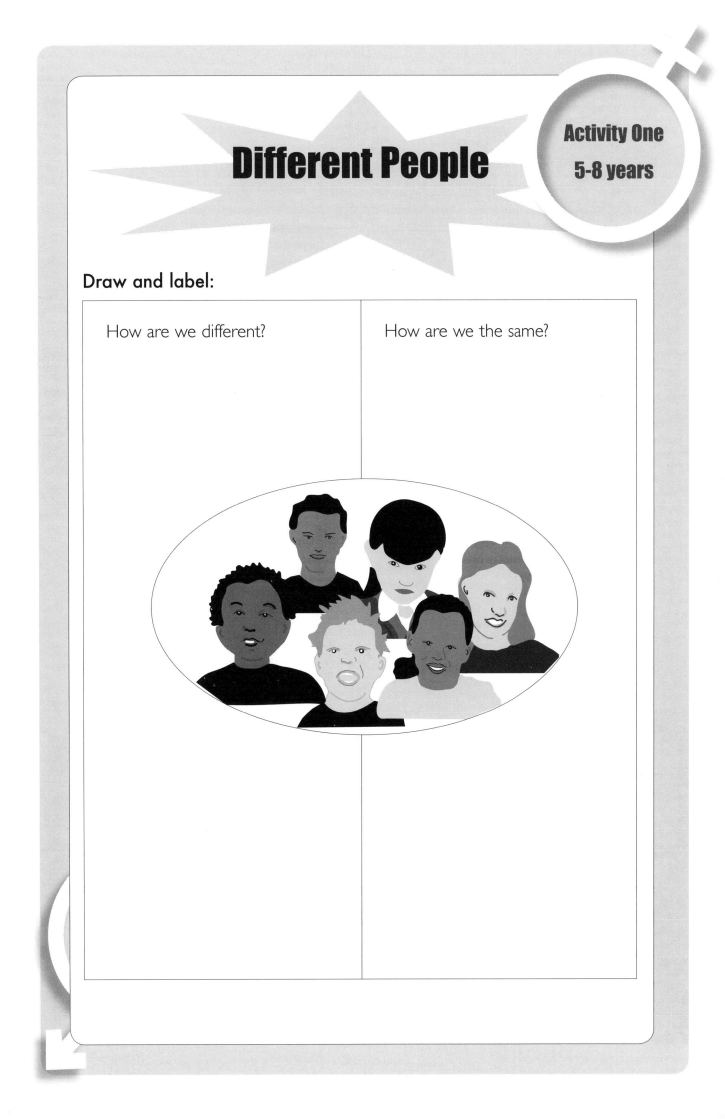

A Quiz

Find out about someone who is different to you. Use the headings below to help you make up some questions.

LANGUAGE

BIRTH

MARRIAGE

DRINK

RELIGION

ART

FOOD

DRESS CODE

Make a poster to show what you have found out.

Guess Who?

Circle Time – Use the pictures to prompt discussion:

- Who is this and what do they do?

- How do they help my family and other people where I live?

- Who would or wouldn't I want to be in the future? Why?

Positive Parents and Carers

Draw and label:

Someone who would be good at looking after me	Someone who would not be good at looking after me

Boys and Girls

Draw a girl playing	Draw a boy playing

Questions for Circle Time discussion:

- How are they different?
- How are they the same?
- What do you play with?
- Do you think boys have to be tough and brave?
- Do you think girls have to be soft and gentle?
- What kind of boy or girl are you?

Our Games

- Circle the games that make you noisy with a red pen.
- Circle the games that make you fight a lot with a green pen.
- Circle the games that make you quiet with a yellow pen.
- Circle the games that make you kind and friendly with a blue pen.

A Problem - Adam's Anger

Cartoon strip of boy in playground

Wants to join in – gets into football game

He gets angry when other team scores

Teacher sees and comes over to send him off the pitch

He turns round and thumps her

Girl from other team scores another goal and pushes him as she does so

Questions for Circle Time discussion:

- Why does Adam get angry at first?
- What makes him feel angrier?
- Is he 'right' to feel angry?
- Why does he thump the girl?
- What will happen next?
- Do you think the girl will hit him back?
- What would help Adam to not hit out?

Make some suggestions.

....

....

....

....

When I Grow Up...

Draw and label what you want to be.

- Compare your job with a friend
- Have boys and girls chosen different jobs?
- Why might they choose different jobs?
- Why might they choose the same jobs?

My World

Cut out the following statement cards.

Place them in order of importance – which influences you the most and which influences you least. Compare your ranking to a friend's and discuss any similarities and differences.

My friends	My teachers
Magazines	My parents / carers
Television	Music
Being a boy / girl	Newspapers
Games / play	Videos / DVD's
Famous people	Popular people
My religion	My culture
My feelings	My brain

My Future

The sky's the limit!

Ask pupils to contribute to the Circle Time session by focusing on the following questions:

- What do I want to do in the future?
- What kind of life do I want to lead?
- How do I want to feel?
- What kind of man or woman do I want to be?
- What is my dream?
- What do I need to do in order to begin to reach my goals?
- Who else can help?
- What TARGETS do I need to set for myself now?

GO FOR IT!

What Do We Know About Our Cultures?

What do we know about our cultures?

Record as many facts as you can. Then consider the following question: How are we similar and how are we different?

Investigation

Find out about another culture. Interview a friend or a member of staff. You can make up a questionnaire and include all the topics that might interest you. The headings in the idea box below may be helpful.

- Language(s).

- Celebrating births and deaths.

- Celebrating marriages.

- Food.

- Drink.

- Role of women.

- Role of men.

- Attitudes towards education/schooling.

- Attitudes towards other cultures.

- Religious beliefs and customs.

- Music.

- Art.

- History.

- Attitude towards children.

- dress code/any 'special' clothing.

Think of a way to present your information that is both original and respectful.

People Who Help

Circle Time – use a selection of pictures to prompt discussion:

- Who is this person and what do they do?

- How do they help me, my family and the wider community?

- What do I feel about their role and which role might I want to adopt later on?

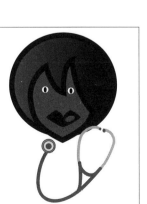

Positive and Negative Parenting

What makes a 'positive' parent or carer? What do they do? How do they communicate? What makes someone a 'negative' parent or carer?

Stop, think, reflect and discuss. Then record your groups' ideas in the two columns below before feeding back to the whole group.

Positive Qualities	Negative Qualities

Boys and Girls

What are they made of?

Sometimes people have tried to make little boys and girls different to each other. They have been rewarded or gain attention for doing different things and behaving in different ways.

BOYS are expected to be:	GIRLS are expected to:
• noisy • aggressive • run around • be tough • be brave • not cry.	• soft and gentle • interested in looking after babies • enjoy tidying up • be pretty • play quietly.

Questions to consider:

- Do you agree with this distinction?
- How did adults treat you when you were little?
- What did you play with?
- Did the games or toys you were given reinforce these characteristics or not?
- Do you think boys have to be tough and brave?
- Do you think girls should be soft and gentle?
- When boys go to school, they are expected to play 'nicely' and 'quietly'.

Do you think this might be difficult for them if they have been allowed to play noisily?

- When girls go to school, they are expected to play 'nicely' and 'quietly'.

Do you think this might limit their ability to learn certain things or in certain subjects?

Investigate Your Games

Tick the boxes which you think fit the games best.

Add your own games to the list.

What are they teaching you? Games / Toys / Activities	Makes you noisy	Makes you fight a lot	Makes you want to be better than others	Makes you look after others	Makes you self conscious and worry about being attractive	Makes you run around	Makes you quiet	Makes you feel happy	Makes you feel friendly
A gun									
A doll									
Nintendo									
A car									
Football									
Make-up									
Tea Set									
Nurses' Outfit									
Boxing Gloves									
Mobile Phone									

When I Grow Up...

Mikey is 7 and is just about to transfer to KS2. He is always in trouble at school because he fights a lot. He gets angry but his dad tells him to be tough and don't cry. He says a man shouldn't show his emotions – only soft blokes do that. But Mikey really wants to talk to someone. But he can't because none of the boys do that sort of thing. He has one girl friend but she's getting fed up with him always being in trouble. His teacher is just angry with him all the time because he can't sit nicely and get on with his work. Mikey feels miserable and doesn't want to go to junior school. He misses his friend Callum who went off to another school at the end of last term when his mum moved house. They used to do a lot of stuff together and Callum helped him to feel calmer by talking to him. He never shouted. He was quiet and kind but Mikey's dad didn't like him. He said Callum would grow up to be a 'poofy hairdresser' or something. Last week Mikey felt so miserable, he bunked off school. He's scared to go in on Monday because they found out and now he's got to go and see the Head with his mum and dad. It's a real mess.

Questions for discussion:

- Why is Mikey always in trouble?
- What do you think of his Dad's views on boys?
- Is it healthy for boys not to talk about their feelings?
- What happens to people when they 'bottle up' their emotions?
- Can a boy be strong and gentle at the same time?
- Can a girl be assertive and gentle at the same time?
- Do you think the adults realise that Mikey is missing his friend so much?
- What do you think Mikey's parents can do to help him?
- What do you think Mikey's teachers can do to help him?
- Can you draw up an 'Action Plan' to help him?

Survey The Group!

What do you want to do in the future? What job or career would you choose now? Ask the people in your group and record their responses on the chart below.

Name of pupil	Job or career chosen	Reason

(Copy additional sheets if necessary)

Discuss – Have girls and boys chosen different or similar careers or jobs?
Can you think why this might be so? Does it have to be like this?